FOR HEALTHY KIDS AND BUSY PARENTS

Wholesome Family Recipes in
30 Minutes or Less From Three Leading
Child Nutrition Experts

Sandra K. Nissenberg, M.S., R.D.

Margaret L. Bogle, Ph.D., R.D.

Audrey C. Wright, M.S., R.D.

JOHN WILEY & SONS, INC.

New York • Chichester • Weinheim • Brisbane • Singapore • Toronto

The information contained in this book is not intended to serve as a replacement for professional medical advice. Any use of the information in this book is at the reader's discretion. The author and the publisher specifically disclaim any and all liability arising directly or indirectly from the use or application of any information contained in this book. A health care professional should be consulted regarding your specific situation.

ISBN 0-471-34698-5

Printed in the United States of America

10

Acknowledgments

I would like to thank Rosalyn Fox, Peggy Mark, Barbara Pearl, and Leslie Nissenberg, who shared ideas and recipes for this book. Thanks also to my children, Heather and Corey, and my husband, Andy, who helped with the taste-testing.

Sandy Nissenberg

Special thanks to my daughters, Laurie Fritz and Laurie Bogle, who contributed some of the recipes after trying them out on my grandchildren.

Margaret Bogle

Sincerest thanks to my daughters, Margaret Dillard, Susan Heindel, daughter-in-law Beth Wright, and my precious grandchildren, who were always willing and ready to try new recipes for me.

Audrey Wright

Table of Contents

About the Authors

Sandra K. Nissenberg, M.S., R.D., is a nutrition consultant in Buffalo Grove, Illinois. She is a former staff member of The American Dietetic Association and its Foundation.

Margaret L. Bogle, Ph.D., R.D., is on the faculty of the Department of Pediatrics, University of Arkansas for Medical Sciences, and Director of Clinical Nutrition and Research, Arkansas Children's Hospital in Little Rock. She has served on the Board of Directors of The American Dietetic Association and its Foundation.

Audrey C. Wright, M.S., R.D., is director of the Father Walter Memorial Child Care Center in Montgomery, Alabama. She has served on the Board of Directors of The American Dietetic Association and is currently president of its Foundation.

Introduction

So many priorities . . . so little time!

How in the world are we supposed to get it all done? We struggle to balance work, family, carpooling, errands, and the other everyday tasks of life, often at the expense of meals and family time. Healthful meals are a priority, but planning time just isn't available.

So . . . what's for dinner?

In times gone by, family meals used to be all-day affairs. The planning, shopping, cooking, and table setting were all detailed, time-consuming events, culminating with the family gathered around the dinner table (all at the same time!) for a leisurely meal and conversation about the day's events and world affairs in general.

Not anymore. Times have changed. Meal planning and cooking have changed as well. But the need for well-planned and healthful meals for the family has not changed.

Our goals in *Quick Meals for Healthy Kids and Busy Parents* are:

- to help you plan quick and healthful meals for your family;

- to provide fun and interesting recipes your family will like;

- to help you organize and simplify your menu planning and food shopping;

- to give you the latest information available on healthful eating for families.

Not only has the way in which meals are organized and planned changed, but the meals themselves have changed. Today, we are becoming more and more aware of the effects of various foods on our health at all ages. Just trying to keep up with that information is time consuming.

New approaches to meals and cooking

Most of the recipes in *Quick Meals* can be prepared in less than 30 minutes, yet offer nutritious, delicious choices for your family. One of the biggest changes in meal preparation in the 90s is the use of one-dish meals instead of the huge meals with multiple courses that used to be the norm. Although we do have quick dishes made from meats, poultry, and fish, we have also collected a variety of one-dish meals, pasta selections, baked potatoes, stir-fried meals, foods wrapped in tortillas, and more. We want to offer a selection of meals that are fun and interesting, yet still wholesome and nutritious.

And, knowing that children are creative and like to help in the kitchen, we have provided many recipes that children can make or help prepare. Since more members of the family tend to be involved in meal preparation in the 90s, the simplicity of our recipes makes that much easier for everyone. Besides, preparing family meals together provides more opportunities for family interaction and fun than simply sitting at the table together.

Making it easy for you

hat exactly does "healthful eating" mean? How can you find out, understand it, and fit it into a schedule that is already impossible? We (the authors) are all registered dietitians and mothers with experience in nutrition and the problems of feeding children and families, as well as the stresses of juggling impossible schedules.

We have organized this book to be as quick and easy as possible for you to use. In the first section, we have included the latest information about healthful eating, including the food pyramid, the new nutrient labeling system now required on foods, and a brief discussion of fat in the diet for adults and children.

We have also provided ideas for organizing your grocery shopping and your kitchen to simplify and speed up the whole process, yet keeping health in mind. We offer ideas on good daily eating habits, snacks, feeding picky eaters, and eating out.

The recipe section brings you nearly 150 easy-to-make recipes. With each recipe, we have included an extensive nutrient analysis that will assist you when selecting recipes. We also offer menu suggestions with each recipe to help you plan delicious and balanced meals. (Recipes for foods marked with an asterisk are included in this book.)

We hope you and your family enjoy *Quick Meals for Healthy Kids and Busy Parents*, not only in enjoying the recipes, but also in having fun just being together!

Sandra K. Nissenberg, M.S., R.D.

Margaret L. Bogle, Ph.D., R.D.

Audrey C. Wright, M.S., R.D.

Tools to help you get started

Healthful eating became easier to understand when the U.S. Department of Agriculture came up with the Food Guide Pyramid in the 1990s. Shortly after, new laws were passed governing food labels. These two actions, along with the continuing emphasis on reducing fat in the diet, have revolutionized the way we think about food and meal planning for our families and ourselves.

At a glance, the Food Guide Pyramid (page 6) shows which foods to eat the most of and which to eat sparingly. Cereals and grains, at the base of the pyramid, are the major focus, while fats, oils, and sugars, which top the pyramid, are to be used least often.

According to the USDA's official food guide pyramid booklet, "the pyramid is an outline of what to eat each day . . . a general guide that lets you choose a healthful diet that is right for you." The basic principles of a healthful diet—variety, balance, and moderation—are still important for everyone.

There are no forbidden foods on the pyramid, and no foods are more important than others. For good health, we need them all. Healthful eating doesn't mean giving up the foods you like best. Instead, it means learning to balance the choices. The pyramid does promote lower-fat diets, however, because Americans tend to eat too much fat and fat is a major factor in many chronic diseases.

Fats, Oils, & Sweets
Use sparingly

Milk, Yogurt, & Cheese Group
2-3 Servings

Meat, Poultry, Fish, Dry Beans, Eggs, & Nut Group
2-3 Servings

Vegetable Group
3-5 Servings

Fruit Group
2-4 Servings

Bread, Cereal, Rice, & Pasta Group
6-11 Servings

How much is a serving?

As with the number of servings, the size of the servings themselves will depend on the same factors (age, gender, activity level). The following chart shows serving sizes for various age groups:

Food Group	Serving Sizes		
	toddler	preschooler	older child or adult
breads & starches			
bread	1/4 slice	1/2 slice	1 slice
rice/pasta	1/4 cup	1/3 cup	1/2 cup
cooked cereal	1/4 cup	1/3 cup	1/2 cup
dry cereal	1/4 cup	1/3 cup	1 oz
fruits			
fresh fruit	2 tbsp	1/4 cup	1 piece
juice	1/4 cup	1/2 cup	3/4 cup
canned fruit	1/4 cup	1/2 cup	1/2 cup
vegetables			
cooked	2 tbsp	1/4 cup	1/2 cup
raw	2 tbsp	1/4 cup	1/2-1 cup
milk & dairy			
milk or yogurt	1/2 cup	3/4 cup	1 cup
cheese	1 oz	1 1/2 oz	1 1/2-2 oz
meat & protein			
lean meat	1 oz	1 1/2 oz	1 1/2-3 oz
cooked beans	2 tbsp	1/4 cup	1/2 cup*
egg	1/2	1	1*
peanut butter	1 tbsp	2 tbsp	2 tbsp*

*Count as 1 oz meat or 1/3 serving from the meat/protein group

How many servings?

The pyramid shows a range of servings for each food group. Individual needs will depend on age, gender, size and level of activity. This table shows how many servings of each major food group can be included at different calorie levels. Preschool children need the same variety of foods as older family members but may need less than 1,600 calories.

Sample food plan for a day

	1,600 calories	2,200 calories	2,800 calories
	For school aged children, sedentary women and some older adults	Most children over the age of 10, teenage girls, active women, and many sedentary men	Teenage boys, many active men, and some very active women
bread group	6	9	11
fruit group	2	3	4
vegetable group	3	4	5
milk group	2-3	2-3	2-3
meat group	5 oz	6 oz	7 oz

How much should I expect my young child to eat?

*C*hildren's appetites vary considerably from day to day and even from one meal to the next, so you shouldn't expect (or demand) a clean plate every meal. It's tough to know how much food you should serve, but a good rule of thumb is 1 tablespoon of each food per year of age up to about age 5. Don't be too concerned that a child gets the right amount of nutrients at each meal or snack. It's more important that nutrient needs are met by averaging intakes over time—over a day or a week.

Suggested meals and snacks

	1 to 3 years	4 to 6 years
breakfast		
milk	1/2 cup	3/4 cup
juice, fruit	1/4 cup	1/2 cup
cereal	1/4 cup	1/3 cup
bread	1/4 to 1/2 slice	1/2 slice
mid-morning/ mid-afternoon snack		
milk	1/2 cup	1/2 cup
bread or	1/4 to 1/2 slice	1/2 cup
graham cracker (2"x 2") or	1	2
vanilla wafers	2	4 to 6

Suggested meals and snacks (continued)

	1 to 3 years	4 to 6 years
lunch or dinner		
milk	1/2 cup	1/2 to 3/4 cup
meat/meat alternative		
poultry, fish, cheese	1 oz	1 1/2 oz
cooked egg	1/2 egg	1 egg
cooked dry beans or peas	2 tbsp	1/4 cup
peanut butter	1 tbsp	2 tbsp
vegetables, fruit	2 tbsp	1/4 to 1/3 cup
breads (whole grain or enriched)	1/4 to 1/2 slice	1/2 slice

Smart snacking

Snacking is vital for young children because of their small stomachs. But be careful not to get into the habit of feeding the little ones all day long. Snacking times should be planned throughout the day, with a beginning and an end just like meals. Allow enough time for your child to be hungry again before offering a snack or meal; 1 1/2 to 2 hours between feedings usually works best for preschoolers.

Children who learn good habits at a young age are likely to continue to follow a good example once they are old enough to make choices for themselves. An occasional treat is not the end of the world and rarely will a child turn down the opportunity to have one, but it should fit into an overall food plan, rather than replace it.

Remember, though, adults usually set the example. If junk foods are brought home and shared nightly in front of the TV, kids are likely to develop some not-so-healthy habits. On the other hand, if a fresh fruit basket is shared instead, children may learn to make healthier choices.

The following list offers ideas for snacks—although this is by no means a complete list.

Finger food snacks

Meat/protein foods

Cold chicken or turkey

Hard cooked eggs

Peanut butter

Milk & dairy foods

Cheese (sticks/cubes)

Cottage cheese

Ice cream

Ice milk, frozen yogurt

Milk shakes

Yogurt

Raw vegetables

(plain or with dip)

Broccoli florets

Carrots/baby carrots

Cauliflower

Celery sticks stuffed with cheese or peanut butter

Cucumber slices

Green beans
Red/yellow or green sweet peppers
Tomato wedges/cherry tomatoes
Turnip slices
Zucchini and yellow squash slices

Fruits

Apple wedges
Banana slices
Grapefruit sections
Melon balls or cubes
Peach or pear slices
Pitted prunes or plums
Raisins or yogurt raisins
Seedless grapes
Soft dried fruit
Strawberry slices

Breads & cereals

Animal crackers
Bread sticks

Finger food snacks (continued)

Breads & cereals

French toast sticks

Fruit-filled cookie bars

Graham crackers

Mini-bagels

Mini-muffins

Oatmeal cookies

Pretzels

Raisin bread

Rice cakes

Toasted bagel or pita chips

Vanilla wafers

New food labels make food choices easier

Trying to figure out what is in various foods, including calories, fat, vitamins, and more, has always been frustrating for consumers. Thanks to new Federal regulations, it is becoming much easier to identify the content and nutritional value of most foods. The new food label system is required on almost all packaged foods.

In addition, words such as fat free, low sodium, light, low cholesterol, and others, now have strict guidelines and definitions that dictate how those terms can be used. For example, in order for the words "fat free" to be used, the food must contain less than 1/2 gram of fat. Another big change is that the serving size for similar types of foods is to be the same, making comparisons easier for consumers.

Look for this heading on food packages.

Nutrition Facts

Serving Size 1/2 cup (114 g)
Servings Per Container 4

The standard serving size and number of servings per container are listed here.

Total calories and calories from fat are listed here.

Amount Per Serving

Calories 260   Calories from Fat 120

	% Daily Value*
Total Fat 13 g	**20%**
Saturated Fat 5 g	**25%**
Cholesterol 30 mg	**10%**
Sodium 660 mg	**28%**
Total Carbohydrate 31 g	**11%**
Dietary Fiber 0 g	**0%**
Sugars 5 g	
Protein 5 g	

% Daily Values indicate how a serving of this food fits into the overall diet. It is based on a 2,000 calorie diet.

Vitamin A 4%	•	Vitamin C 2%
Calcium 15%	•	Iron 4%

*Percent Daily Values are based on a 2,000 calorie diet. Your daily values may be higher or lower depending on your calorie needs:

Nutrient requirements are listed here for a 2,000 and 2,500 calorie diet. Your levels may vary based on specific needs.

	Calories	2,000	2,500
Total Fat	Less than	65 g	80 g
Sat Fat	Less than	20 g	25 g
Cholesterol	Less than	300 mg	300 mg
Sodium	Less than	2400 mg	2400 mg
Total Carbohydrate		300 g	375 g
Dietary Fiber		25 g	30 g

Calories per gram:

Fat 9 • Carbohydrate 4 • Protein 4

This information is a reminder of how many calories are in a gram of fat, carbohydrate, and protein.

These quick-reference tools—the Food Guide Pyramid, the sample food plan chart based on serving size and calorie levels, the serving size chart, and the new food labels—are all geared to helping consumers make healthful food choices for themselves and their families.

Protecting your family from too much fat

In our culture, fat might as well be a four-letter word. But the truth is, fat has been given a bum rap in some ways. It is a nutrient and, as such, plays some very important roles in maintaining health.

The concentrated calories in fat make it easier to meet children's energy needs, even when their capacity for food is small. The fat soluble vitamins (especially A, D, E, and K) are essential for growing children. And the so-called "high-fat" foods (milk, red meat, and eggs) contain many other vitamins and minerals not found in the same quantities in other foods. So we all need fat—but just not as much as many of us get.

Should we be watching how much fat our children eat? The answer is both yes and no. Fat should not be restricted in children under age 2 unless a doctor specifically recommends cutting fat. From birth to age 2, most children need extra fat because of their rapid growth. It is important at this age that children experience a variety of foods and begin to learn healthful eating habits.

For the rest of us over age 2, the Dietary Guidelines for Americans recommend limiting fat in our diets to 30 percent of calories.

In many cases, fat can be cut by following a few simple tips. Most recipes can be prepared with fat substitutes without sacrificing taste. In looking at the following list of tips for reducing fat, remember that fat should be averaged over an entire meal, a day, or week at a time.

Tips for reducing fat in recipes

- Use skim, 1%, or 2% milk in cooking instead of whole milk.

- Remove all visible fat from meat, chicken or turkey before cooking.

- Select only "lean" cuts of meat.

- Ask about the percentage of fat in ground beef, pork, chicken or turkey.

- Use the lower fat percentage ground meats.

- Use fruit juices to baste roasts, fish or other meats instead of butter, margarine or drippings from the meat.

- Broil (on a rack so drippings can be discarded), boil, steam or poach meats and vegetables instead of frying in oil or shortening.

- Pan broil meats and vegetables by coating the skillet or pan with vegetable oil cooking spray and use pans with non-stick surfaces.

- Let meat drippings get cold so that more fat can be removed after it solidifies.

- After boiling a chicken or other meat, let the broth get cold and then skim the solid fat off.

- Use reduced-fat varieties of ingredients instead of the higher fat originals, such as low-fat sour cream, cream cheese, other cheeses and yogurt.

- Use cheeses that are made from skim or part-skim milk.

- Use the white of an egg instead of the whole egg in many recipes.

- Egg substitutes may be used in many recipes for whole eggs.

- Applesauce can be substituted for half of the butter, margarine, oil, and other fats in many recipes.

Getting your family to try new foods

Does your house turn into a battleground when you offer a new food to your children? Is it easier for you to give them what they want instead of trying new foods and recipes? When given a choice does your child want the same old food over and over again?

If these are concerns in your home, don't panic. This is common for many of us. So what should we do?

First, look at your own eating habits. Children learn their habits from the adults they live with. When they observe good habits, they develop good habits and tend to be better eaters throughout their lives. Of course, the opposite applies too.

Everyone has special likes and dislikes, and your favorites can't be pushed on your family. If one item or one meal doesn't please the family, try another. Or try preparing the food a different way. But try to always offer good choices.

It's not uncommon for young children to go on food jags where they want the same food every single day. The foods most commonly asked for are peanut butter sandwiches, macaroni and cheese, dry cereal, and so on. These are all nutritious foods for children, so don't be too concerned. You may be bored with the preparation, but the kids will soon move on to something else.

If you are concerned about offering a wider variety, make small changes that might appeal to your child. For example, offer peanut butter and applesauce or peanut butter and banana sandwiches in a tortilla. Or try a new cereal. If you still find yourself with a stubborn child and the food jags persist—they can go on for months at a time—continue to offer other fun, colorful, and creative choices.

The more opportunities your child has to experiment with and taste various foods, the more he or she will enjoy and be willing to try new foods. Make the experiences pleasant ones. Don't force or bribe a youngster to eat. You will only set yourself up for unpleasant mealtimes and foster negative attitudes toward food.

When offering new foods, try to:

- Set good examples by serving everyone the same foods and eating those foods yourself.

- Offer new foods at the beginning of a meal, when your child is most hungry.

- Present new foods with at least one food your child already likes.

Some other important points to keep in mind are:

- Your responsibility is to provide a variety of healthy, nutritious foods; your child's responsibility is to eat them.

- Don't punish, force, or bribe your child with food.

- Don't console your child with food. It isn't something that we want tied with our emotions at an early age.

- Set house rules: You don't have to eat it all, just taste one bite.

- Start with small portions and let him ask for more if he desires.

- Let your child fill his or her plate from the choices available. Ask the whole family to take only what they will eat.

- Allow your child to help with meal preparation and table setting. Mealtime is more interesting if everyone has had a role in preparing for it.

When your child refuses a certain food, here are some options to try instead.

If your child doesn't like...

Red meat

Try instead
Eggs, poultry, fish, peanut butter, dried beans or peas

Why?
These are not as tough and difficult to chew.
They are also good protein sources.

What else can you do?
Cut meat into tiny pieces. Use cooking methods that tenderize
tough meats, such as marinating.

If your child doesn't like...

Green vegetables

Try instead
Orange or yellow vegetables: carrots, squash, corn, sweet potatoes

Why?
These are not as bitter. They have a comparable nutrient value.

What else can you do?
Offer raw vegetables with dip.

If your child doesn't like...

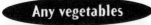
Any vegetables

Try instead
Fruits: apple, banana, pear, grapes, cantaloupe, watermelon

Why?
They have a comparable nutrient value.

What else can you do?
Try fruit and vegetable juices.

If your child doesn't like...

Milk

Try instead
Yogurt, cheese, pudding, cottage cheese,
or flavored (chocolate, strawberry) milk

Why?
These are also good calcium sources.

What else can you do?
Incorporate milk into food preparation.
(Add milk to scrambled eggs, soups, etc.)

When your child just isn't hungry

*P*robably the greatest frustration to most parents is a child's complete lack of appetite. One thing for sure, though: A child will eat when she or he is hungry. Over time, children even out their food intake, averaging the same calories every day.

It's not necessary to force your child to eat. In fact, coercing will merely increase resistance. And you will only set yourself up for frustrating mealtimes. You may even notice your child eats more when you put less emphasis on the meal.

Don't assume your child is picky or particular about foods if she or he rejects a certain food. Some foods might be difficult to chew or might be unappealing because of the color or smell. We all go through this, even as adults. When something doesn't work, make a mental note to change the way you serve it next time.

Grocery shopping

*C*hildren sometimes look at food shopping as an adventure, while tired and frustrated parents may not feel the same. If this is true for you, try to make your trip as short as possible by being prepared. With meals in mind, prepare your list and coupons.

When you enter the store begin by telling your child that you are not at the supermarket to eat. Try to make the trip as pleasant as possible. You can even make it educational.

Ask your child to help you put foods into the cart or select light-weight items from the shelves. Encourage youngsters to help to choose fruits, vegetables, shapes of pasta, or flavors of frozen yogurt. Children tend to be more interested in eating what they have helped to select.

Drive a smart cart. Buy . . .

- lots of fruits and vegetables

- milk, cheeses, cottage cheese and yogurt

- lean ground beef, chicken, turkey and fish

- frozen yogurt and ice milk

- unsweetened breakfast cereals

- mini rice cakes, bagels and pretzels

- deli-sliced or shaved turkey breast and lean roast beef

- whole wheat or mixed grain breads

Tips for stocking your shelves

It's easy to get frustrated choosing what to make for dinner. Your day has been busy. The time to decide is now at hand. Most likely, a look in your pantry will determine your meal.

A fully stocked pantry will make it easier to prepare and serve a healthy meal with the least amount of effort. Quick meals can be just as nutritious as those that require lengthy preparation time. Basically, it's all dependent on what foods or staples you have and the time you have for preparation.

We have listed some suggestions for stocking your pantry, freezer, and refrigerator that can make your meal preparation a pleasure rather than a stressful situation.

Keep in dry storage

Beans, dried and canned

Bouillon, chicken and beef

Breads, whole grain and enriched

Crackers

Flour, enriched and whole grain

Fruits canned in juice

Herbs and spices, dried onions

Honey

Oils, vegetable and olive

Onions

Pasta in a variety of shapes and sizes

Potatoes

Rice, quick cooking, white and brown

Sauces, barbecue, soy, catsup, spaghetti

Sugar, white and brown

Tomatoes, whole and sauce, canned

Tuna and salmon, water packed

Keep in your freezer

Bagels, pita bread
Boneless chicken breasts
Fish fillets
Frozen vegetables, fruits and fruit juices
Lean beef, ground or roast
Pizza crust

Keep in your refrigerator

Canned breadsticks
Canned pizza dough
Citrus juice, orange or grapefruit
Cottage cheese
Dijon mustard
Fresh fruits in season
Lemons
Milk, low-fat
Salad dressings, light or low-fat
Salsa
Vegetables, carrots, celery, lettuce, green pepper, tomatoes
Yogurt

Pyramid your pantry

The Food Guide Pyramid is a wonderful tool to help you eat a more nutritious diet. But many people still have trouble combining foods to prepare healthy meals. To help, you may want to organize your pantry accordingly.

Pretend your pantry illustrates the pyramid. Start by taping a copy of the pyramid on the inside of your pantry door. Then begin with the bottom shelf.

Place all grain, pasta, cracker, cereal and bread items on the bottom shelf.

Move up to the next shelf for fruits and vegetables. Obviously, many of these need to go in the refrigerator, but the canned and dried fruits and canned vegetables can be shelved together.

The next shelf up is for protein-rich foods, such as canned tuna, chicken, salmon; dried beans, peas, and legumes, dry milk powder, and pudding mixes.

On the top shelf (don't leave too much space), place your oils, cooking fats, cake mixes, cookies, and candies.

You can also organize your refrigerator in a similar pattern.

When you begin to plan your meal, start at the bottom shelf and then choose an item from each shelf. Combine foods to complete your pyramid. You are now on your way to a healthier diet.

Bring back family meals

Food is to be enjoyed. Eating with others, family, and friends, enhances this enjoyment. It's even been shown that food is digested better when eaten in a relaxed and fun atmosphere.

Family meals of the past provided an excellent opportunity to get to know each other. Much more than food was shared. Family values, the development of communication and interpersonal skills, the development of self worth and self esteem were nurtured in family meals.

Our lives have become more complex. And our food has been undergoing many technological changes, making it easier to prepare meals quickly—hopefully giving families more time to spend together. Time saving equipment, especially the microwave and convection ovens, now allows many foods to be prepared quickly. Family meals now often involve fast food, which is fine as long as family members eat together and share.

You can stop at the delicatessen or grocery and pick up an entree, bread, fresh fruit, and fresh or frozen vegetables. In ten minutes or less, you can transfer the purchased entree to your dishes and cut up a salad while frozen vegetables cook in the microwave. Or you can order a pizza or Chinese food and prepare a salad before the main meal arrives.

This is also the time to involve the children in the preparation of the family meal—either in selecting the fruits or vegetables for a salad, mixing the salad, or setting the table. Children of all ages enjoy eating more when they have been involved in the food and meal preparation.

Remember the important step to family meals is bringing families together. It gives families a purpose. It doesn't mean all meals must be at home or around a table. These meals could be picnics at the ballpark or soccer field where as many family members as possible can eat together and still participate in events with the other children. Where it happens or what food is consumed is secondary. Enjoy and get to know each other.

Eating out

E ating out is part of our lives—whether it's at a fancy restaurant or at a fast food drive-thru. Sometimes we enjoy the time spent away from our kitchens and other times we wonder if going out is even worth the effort (and cost).

To make eating out as enjoyable as it should be, try these suggestions:

- Select informal family-style restaurants where children are welcome and comfortable.

- Plan mealtimes to suit your child's eating schedule.

- Ask for a children's menu. If one is not available, allow your children to share an adult-sized meal or ask for a half-sized serving.

- Never force a child to try a new food when eating out.

- Ask how foods are prepared to make sure they are to your (and your child's) liking.

- Ask that beverages be served with the meal and not before. Sometimes children fill up on drinks before the meal even arrives.

Making wise fast food choices

As you know, meals at fast food restaurants are quick, but they're not always nutritious. However, there are ways to make it fit into a healthy lifestyle.

- Order hamburgers with lettuce and tomatoes or roast beef and turkey sandwiches instead of double hamburgers with sauce or bacon cheeseburgers.

- Select pizza with vegetable toppings rather than sausage and pepperoni.

- Baked potatoes and cole slaw make better choices than french fries and onion rings.

- Choose milk or juice instead of soft drinks.

- Opt for salad bars when available, even for kids.

- Look for skinless, broiled chicken sandwiches in place of fried nuggets.

And, remember to compensate for any nutritional shortcomings of fast food by eating and serving healthier meals and snacks during other times of the day.

Lunch box ideas

$\mathcal{R}$emember that children of all ages respond to peer pressure and may not eat foods away from home that they would at home. Sometimes this turns out for the child's best interests. With friends, most children will eat or experiment with new foods that they will not touch at home, even with parents' urging and role modeling. Take advantage of this opportunity. Find out what other children are eating when your child must "carry" food. Even very young children "share" the contents of their lunch boxes, and few people want to be so different as to stand out. Include one new food or one less favorite food with foods you know your child will eat.

The lunch box or bag should contain a variety of foods, shapes, and textures—the same as meals at home. However, some foods pack and travel better than others. Be aware also that flavors from one food can overshadow a less flavorful one if kept in a closed container together.

Usually children will prefer foods that can be eaten with their fingers. This makes fruit, raw vegetables, and sandwiches well suited for the lunch box. Occasionally, sending soup or chili (especially in the winter) in a thermos can improve lagging appetites.

Even though sandwiches are the traditional lunch choices, other high-protein options include turkey or chicken slices or nuggets, meatloaf, hard cooked eggs, and cheese slices, chunks, or sticks.

If you choose to send sandwiches, instead of bread, try pita pockets, rice cakes, tortillas, muffins, bagels, English muffins, or raisin bread. Experiment with different fillings for the sandwiches: peanut butter and grated carrots, mashed bananas, or raisins; cheeses other than just American; various cooked vegetable purees or fruit purees mixed with low-fat cream cheese; and mixtures of meats, chicken, or tuna fish that includes raw fruits and vegetable pieces to give that extra crunch.

One note of caution about using mixtures of foods in the summer time. Unless the lunch can be refrigerated until eaten, you must be very careful to send only those foods and mixtures that will not spoil easily. This means avoiding mixtures with salad dressing, mayonnaise, or egg- or milk-based sauces.

Cut sandwiches in small (1/4 slice of bread) pieces or strips for easy handling. Or be creative by using various cookie cutters to create sandwiches in the shape of hearts, stars, or even Mickey Mouse or other animals.

Raw fruits and vegetables are great to include. Make them easy to eat by cutting in small pieces, peeling off the skin, etc. For treats, oatmeal raisin or peanut butter cookies, graham or animal crackers, vanilla wafers or fruited mini-muffins can add much nutritional value. In addition, there are many commercial single serving products available, such as Jell-O®, puddings, fruit sauces, sliced fruits, etc. Each comes in its own container, which can be thrown away or recycled after the food is eaten.

Don't forget to include a surprise—either a favorite food or a note, sticker, or cartoon—anything that says, "You are special and I care for you." Your child and his or her friends will look forward to your lunches packed with such love and nutrition.

Have fun with food

The best way to get your child to try new foods and experiment with food is to have fun with it. Creativity and food presentation makes a statement with adults as well as children. There's no question that a variety of foods placed on a lovely plate at a place setting is more appealing than eating a meal in its baking dish. Everyone likes to see attractive, colorful, and appealing foods placed in front of them.

Start off by letting children have fun with foods early on. Buy special plates for your kids. Let them buy or make special placemats. Let them use child-sized utensils and cups.

Look for cookbooks written for children. Many foods can be made without baking and others need only minimal adult supervision. Once your child is old enough to prepare foods himself, let him contribute to tonight's meal. He will be so proud of his creations, he will be more likely to eat them.

It's not necessary to purchase a cookbook to be creative. And there are many ways to have fun with food even if you do not think you're creative. Here's how:

- Use cookie cutters to make sandwiches or to cut square slices of cheese into shapes.

- Let your child decorate sandwiches with raisins, apples, banana slices, or grapes.

- Plain ice cream cones make a nice alternative to bread. Try filling some with tuna or chicken salad or cottage cheese. Top with a grape or cherry tomato.

- Pizzas are fun. They can be made on pita bread, tortillas, English muffins, or bagels. Add spaghetti sauce and whatever vegetables you like. Top with mozzarella cheese and bake. Fruit pizzas, too, are appealing when made with cream cheese and cut up fruit.

- Try meatloaf muffins instead of standard meatloaf. Top each meat-muffin with mashed potatoes and add an olive, cherry tomato, or green peas. Also, stab those meatballs with Popsicle® sticks.

- Make decorative straws by cutting shapes from paper plates. Punch holes in the top and bottom and thread through the straw. It's amazing how much better milk tastes through a fun straw.

It is important that you spend time in the kitchen with your child and have fun with food, too. These are the moments that will make family memories last a lifetime.

Start with a Soup

Dump Soup

Great treat on a cold day as children come home from school.

1 pound lean ground beef
2 10 3/4-ounce cans minestroni soup
16-ounce can ranch-style beans
2 16-ounce cans stewed tomatoes
15-ounce can whole kernel corn
1 cup frozen hash brown potatoes

Brown ground beef and drain off drippings. Combine ground beef with remaining ingredients in medium size soup pot. Heat over medium heat until mixture boils. Reduce heat and simmer about 15 minutes.

If soup appears too thick, add a small amount of warm water.

Servings: 16 (3/4 cup)
172 calories per serving; 11 gm. protein; 23 gm. carbohydrates;
3 gm. fat; 22 mg. cholesterol; 3 gm. fiber; 3 mg. iron;
35 mg. calcium; 694 mg. sodium

Exchanges
1 bread, 1 meat, 1/2 vegetable, 1/2 fat

To balance your meal add: Whole Wheat Crackers,
*Danish Apple Pie

*Recipe included in this book

Oriental Chicken Soup

As a main course, this hearty soup serves any appetite, especially on a cold day. It's also a great way to use leftover chicken.

3 14 1/2-ounce cans chicken broth (regular, unsalted or a combination of both)
1 tbsp. soy sauce
1 tbsp. lemon juice
1/2 tsp. ginger
2 cups frozen vegetables (mixed, cauliflower, broccoli, carrots, or any combination)
1 cup cooked egg noodles
2 1/2 cups cooked chicken, cut up

In large saucepan, combine broth, soy sauce, lemon juice, and ginger. Bring to boil. Add vegetables and noodles. Reduce heat. Add chicken. Cover and simmer for 10 minutes until vegetables are tender and chicken is heated through.

Servings: 6 (1 cup)
180 calories per serving; 21 gm. protein; 16 gm. carbohydrates; 3 gm. fat; 41 mg. cholesterol; 3 gm. fiber; 2 mg. iron; 34 mg. calcium; 1175 mg. sodium

Exchanges
1/2 bread, 2 meat, 1 1/2 vegetable

To balance your meal add: Toasted Buttered Whole Wheat Bread Squares, Fruit Cocktail

Two Potato Soup

Your family will think you spent all day on this one.
It's nutritious, delicious, and perfect on a cool evening.

3 medium white potatoes, peeled and chopped
1 large sweet potato, peeled and chopped
1 onion, chopped
1 3/4 cups chicken broth
1 tsp. dill weed
1 1/2 cups low-fat milk

Place chopped potatoes and onion in large saucepan. Add chicken broth and dill weed. Cook on medium-high heat until boiling. Reduce heat to low. Cover and simmer about 20 minutes until potatoes are soft. Mash potatoes with a potato masher or place mixture in an electric blender or food processor. Mash or blend until potatoes are thoroughly mashed. Add milk. Serve.

Servings: 6 (1 cup)
144 calories per serving; 5 gm. protein; 29 gm. carbohydrates;
1 gm. fat; 5 mg. cholesterol; 2 gm. fiber; 1 mg. iron;
95 mg. calcium; 270 mg. sodium

Exchanges
1 1/2 bread, 1/2 vegetable

*To balance your meal add: *Confetti Chicken Salad, Crackers*

*Recipe included in this book

Cauliflower Potato Soup

Try this delicious soup with broccoli, too.

10-ounce package frozen cauliflower
1/2 cup water
2 10 3/4-ounce cans condensed cream of potato soup
2 cups low-fat milk
1/2 cup cheese, Swiss or cheddar, shredded
1/8 tsp. nutmeg

In large saucepan, combine cauliflower and water. Bring to boil. Reduce heat. Cover and simmer 5 minutes.

Stir in potato soup, milk, cheese, and nutmeg. Cook over medium heat 2 to 3 minutes until thoroughly heated.

Servings: 6 (1 cup)
143 calories per serving; 7 gm. protein; 15 gm. carbohydrates;
6 gm. fat; 19 mg. cholesterol; 1 gm. fiber; 1 mg. iron;
209 mg. calcium; 882 mg. sodium

Exchanges
1/2 bread, 1/2 meat, 1/2 vegetable, 1/2 milk, 1 fat

To balance your meal add: Peanut Butter and Banana Sandwich,
Applesauce in Jell-O®

Italian Vegetable Soup

There are many variations to this soup that are also tasty. Try adding cooked chicken or shrimp and make it a complete meal.

2 tsp. vegetable oil
1/2 cup onion, chopped
1/2 cup celery, chopped
2 garlic cloves, minced
1 tsp. dried basil
1/4 tsp. pepper
1 cup water
10 3/4-ounce can condensed chicken broth
14 1/2-ounce can stewed tomatoes
1 cup frozen corn
2 ounces uncooked spaghetti or pasta
2 tbsp. Parmesan cheese

Heat oil in large skillet or saucepan over medium-high heat. Stir-fry onion, celery, and garlic until vegetables are tender-crisp. Add basil, pepper, water, broth and tomatoes. Bring to boil. Reduce heat. Cover and simmer for 5 minutes. Add corn and pasta. Cover and simmer an additional 10 minutes until pasta is tender. Pour soup into serving bowls. Garnish each bowl with Parmesan cheese.

Servings: 6 (1 cup)
89 calories per serving; 5 gm. protein; 11 gm. carbohydrates;
3 gm. fat; 2 mg. cholesterol; 2 gm. fiber; 1 mg. iron;
48 mg. calcium; 478 mg. sodium

Exchanges
1/2 bread, 1/2 meat, 1/2 fat

*To balance your meal add: *Parmesan Garlic Bread,*
*Apple Pudding

*Recipe included in this book

Chicken, Fish, and More

Dutch Oven Chicken

A one-dish meal that's sure to become a family favorite.

3 pounds chicken pieces, skinless
1/2 tsp. each salt and pepper
1/2 cup flour
1 tbsp. margarine
10 3/4-oz. can condensed cream of
    mushroom soup
1/2 soup can water
1/4 tsp. paprika

Preheat oven to 300°. Sprinkle chicken with salt, pepper, and flour. Place margarine in Dutch oven or covered oven baking pan. Add chicken. Combine soup with water, stirring well. Pour over chicken. Sprinkle with paprika. Bake for 45 minutes.

Servings: 8
283 calories per serving; 38 gm. protein; 9 gm. carbohydrates;
10 gm. fat; 119 mg. cholesterol; 0 fiber; 2 mg. iron;
33 mg. calcium; 590 mg. sodium

Exchanges:
1/2 bread, 3 1/2 meat, 1/2 fat

To balance your meal add: Mashed Potatoes, Sliced Tomatoes
with Dressing, *Chewy Oatmeal Chocolate Cookies

*Recipe included in this book

Golden Baked Chicken

Make your own "Shake it then bake it."

6 chicken breasts, boneless, skinless
1/2 cup flour
1 tbsp. paprika
2 tbsp. margarine
salt and pepper to taste

Preheat oven to 350°. Place flour and paprika in a resealable bag. Add chicken to bag and shake.

Melt margarine in baking dish. Place chicken in baking dish. Cover with aluminum foil. Bake for 20 minutes.

Remove foil. Bake for an additional 10 minutes on each side until chicken is golden brown.

Servings: 6 (1 breast)
204 calories per serving; 29 gm. protein; 9 gm. carbohydrates;
5 gm. fat; 68 mg. cholesterol; 1 gm. fiber; 2 mg. iron;
18 mg. calcium; 122 mg. sodium

Exchanges:
1/2 bread, 3 meat

To balance your meal add: *Spicy Oven Fried Potatoes,
*Apple Fruit Salad, Ice Milk

*Recipe included in this book

Hawaiian Chicken Breasts

This dish is great served over rice. Prepare the rice while your chicken is simmering, and your meal will be done in no time.

4 chicken breasts, boneless, skinless
1 egg, slightly beaten
3/4 cup bread crumbs
1 tsp. salt
2 tbsp. margarine
1 cup pineapple juice
2 tbsp. lemon juice
1 tbsp. cornstarch
1 tbsp. sugar
Slivered almonds, optional

Dip chicken breasts in egg, then roll in bread crumbs. Season with salt.

Melt margarine in skillet. Brown chicken. Pour off excess fat. Add juices, cornstarch and sugar to skillet. Cover and simmer for 20 to 25 minutes. Top with almonds, if desired.

Servings: 4 (1 breast each)
332 calories per serving; 32 gm. protein; 29 gm. carbohydrates;
9 gm. fat; 121 mg. cholesterol; 1 gm fiber; 2 mg. iron;
74 mg. calcium; 856 mg. sodium

Exchanges:
1 bread, 3 meat, 1 fruit

*To balance your meal add: Buttered Rice, English Peas,
Homemade Chocolate Pudding

Nifty Crispy Oven Chicken Drumsticks

*Children love chicken drumsticks. Here's a quick way to make a
crispy version they will love, even if it takes a little extra time.
You can also try it on other chicken pieces too.*

3-oz. can chow mein noodles
2 tbsp. margarine
2 tbsp. honey
1 tbsp. lemon juice
2 tsp. soy sauce
8 chicken drumsticks or thighs

*Recipe included in this book

Preheat oven to 375°. Put chow mein noodles into plastic bag. Using a rolling pin, crush noodles.

Melt margarine. Add honey, lemon juice, and soy sauce. Mix well.

Wash chicken pieces well. Pat dry with paper towel. Using a pastry brush, brush chicken with butter-honey mixture. Roll each in crushed noodles until coated.

Place chicken in 13" x 9" x 2" baking dish. Sprinkle any extra crumbs over top. Bake 1 hour or until chicken is tender.

Servings: 8 (1 drumstick)
216 calories per serving; 15 gm. protein; 11 gm. carbohydrates;
12 gm. fat; 59 mg. cholesterol; 0 fiber; 1 mg. iron;
12 mg. calcium; 227 mg. sodium

Exchanges:
1/2 bread, 2 meat, 1/2 fat

*To balance your meal add: *Chinese Rice,*
*Strawberry Salad, *Vanilla Tea Cookies

*Recipe included in this book

Homemade Chicken Nuggets

Serve these with dipping sauces such as barbecue, honey mustard, applesauce or ranch-style salad dressing.

3 chicken breasts, boneless, skinless
2/3 cup wheat germ
1/2 tsp. salt
1/4 tsp. garlic powder
1/8 tsp. black pepper
1/2 cup water
1 egg white, slightly beaten
Vegetable oil cooking spray

Preheat oven to 400°. Cut up chicken pieces and set aside. Combine wheat germ, salt, garlic powder, and pepper. Place mixture in large plastic bag.

Combine water and egg white in a bowl. Dip chicken into egg mixture, then drop into plastic bag. Shake until chicken is thoroughly coated.

Place chicken pieces in baking dish sprayed with vegetable oil cooking spray. Bake 10 to 15 minutes or until tender and golden brown.

Servings: 6 (3-4 nuggets)
74 calories per serving; 11 gm. protein; 4 gm. carbohydrates;
1 gm. fat; 22 mg. cholesterol; 1 gm. fiber; 1 mg. iron;
8 mg. calcium; 212 mg. sodium

Exchanges:
1/2 bread, 1 meat

*To balance your meal add: *Orange Yams, *Lima Beans in
Sour Cream, *Peanut Butter Oatmeal Cookies*

Parmesan Chicken Nuggets

*Quick and easy to make, and more nutritious
than the ones at a fast food restaurants.*

3 tbsp. margarine
1/4 cup dry bread crumbs
1/4 cup Parmesan cheese
1 tbsp. parsley
2 cloves garlic, minced
2 tsp. Dijon mustard
1 pound chicken breasts, boneless, skinless

Recipe included in this book

In large skillet over medium heat, melt 1 tbsp. of the margarine. Add bread crumbs. Stir until lightly browned. Remove from heat and transfer into small bowl. Add Parmesan cheese and parsley.

Cut chicken into cubes or strips. Melt remaining margarine in skillet. Add garlic, mustard and chicken. Sauté 5 to 10 minutes until chicken is cooked throughout.

Remove chicken with slotted spoon. Toss with bread crumb mixture.

Servings: 12 (3-4 nuggets)
86 calories per serving; 10 gm. protein; 2 gm. carbohydrates;
4 gm. fat; 23 mg. cholesterol; 0 fiber; 0 iron;
42 mg. calcium; 136 mg. sodium

Exchanges:
1 meat

*To balance your meal add: Pasta with Tomato Sauce, Mixed Green Salad, *Quick and Easy Carrot Cake*

Recipe included in this book

Barbecue Chicken and Rice

Try this nutritious and colorful one-dish meal tonight.

> 1 pound chicken breasts, boneless, skinless
> 2 tbsp. vegetable oil
> 1 1/2 cups barbecue sauce
> 1 cup water
> 11-oz. can whole kernel corn, drained
> 1 small green pepper, chopped
> 1 small red pepper, chopped
> 2 cups instant rice, uncooked

Slice chicken breasts into strips or chunks. Heat oil in large skillet and brown chicken. Stir in barbecue sauce, water, corn, and peppers. Bring to boil. Reduce heat. Cover and simmer 5 minutes.

Remove from heat. Add rice and cover. Let stand 5 minutes until rice is fluffy.

Servings: 8 (3/4 cup)
255 calories per serving; 17 gm. protein; 35 gm. carbohydrates;
5 gm. fat; 33 mg. cholesterol; 2 gm. fiber; 2 mg. iron;
24 mg. calcium; 546 mg. sodium

Exchanges:
1 1/2 bread, 1 1/2 meat, 1 vegetable, 1 fat

To balance your meal add: *Danish Apple Pie

*Recipe included in this book

Chicken and Vegetable Pasta

*This dish will inspire compliments for its taste
and colorful appearance.*

2 tbsp. vegetable oil
1 cup broccoli, chopped
1/2 cup onion, chopped
2 cloves garlic, minced
1 carrot, thinly sliced
1 celery stalk, thinly sliced
2 cups cooked chicken, cut up
16-oz. can chopped tomatoes
4 cups cooked pasta (any shape)
1/4 cup Parmesan cheese
1 tsp. parsley, optional

In large skillet over medium heat, heat oil. Stir-fry broccoli, onion, garlic, carrot, and celery. Add chicken and tomatoes. Cook until heated through, about 5 minutes.

While chicken is cooking, prepare pasta according to package directions.

Spoon chicken and vegetables over hot pasta. Sprinkle with Parmesan cheese and parsley, if desired.

Servings: 6 (1 cup each)
269 calories per serving; 17 gm. protein; 34 gm. carbohydrates;
8 gm. fat; 28 mg. cholesterol; 4 gm. fiber; 2 mg. iron;
105 mg. calcium; 237 mg. sodium

Exchanges:
1 1/2 bread, 1 meat, 1 vegetable, 1 fat

To balance your meal add: Chilled Pineapple Slices,
*Peanut Butter Pudding

*Recipe included in this book

Chicken and Rice A Roni

My grandchildren like this when I add 1/2 can cooked, chopped carrots. Other vegetables can be added too. Other meats, like chopped ham or tuna fish, can be substituted for the chicken.

7.2-oz. box Rice a Roni®, any flavor
5-oz. can white meat chicken
10 3/4-oz. can cream of chicken soup
10 3/4-oz. can cream of mushroom soup

Cook Rice a Roni according to package directions. Add chicken and soups. Heat thoroughly for 10 minutes. Serve hot.

Servings: 10 (1/2 cup)
102 calories per serving; 5 gm. protein; 13 gm. carbohydrates;
3 gm. fat; 9 mg. cholesterol; 0 fiber; 1 mg. iron;
14 mg. calcium; 474 mg. sodium

Exchanges:
1/2 bread, 1/2 meat, 1 fat

*To balance your meal add: *Garlic Green Beans, *Fruit Ambrosia*

Recipe included in this book

Golden Baked Fish Fillet

Children love this easy and nutritious fish dish.

1/2 cup low-fat milk
1 tsp. salt
1 1/2 cups slightly crushed cornflakes
1 pound fish fillets
2 tbsp. margarine, melted

Preheat oven to 400°. Pour milk in small bowl. Add salt. In another small bowl, pour in cornflake crumbs. Dip fish fillets in milk and then into crumbs. Place in baking dish and dot with melted margarine.

Bake for 20 minutes until fish flakes easily with a fork.

Servings: 4 (4 ounces)
239 calories per serving; 26 gm. protein; 12 gm. carbohydrates;
9 gm. fat; 39 mg. cholesterol; 0 fiber; 2 mg. iron;
93 mg. calcium; 789 mg. sodium

Exchanges:
1/2 bread, 4 meat, 1 fat

To balance your meal add: *Easy Rice Souffle,
*Oriental Spinach, *Chewy Chocolate Brownies

*Recipe included in this book

Oven Poached Fish

Quick and delicious! A great choice for a last minute meal.

1 pound fish steaks or fillets (any type of fish)
1 tsp. lemon juice
1/4 tsp. pepper
1/2 tsp. dill weed
1/4 cup dry white wine

Preheat oven to 425°. Place fish in medium baking dish. Sprinkle with lemon juice, pepper, and dill. Pour wine in bottom of pan. Bake 20-25 minutes until fish flakes easily with fork. Serve immediately.

Servings: 4 (4 ounces)
114 calories per serving; 21 gm. protein; 0 carbohydrates;
1 gm. fat; 54 mg. cholesterol; 0 fiber; 1 mg. iron;
25 mg. calcium; 93 mg. sodium

Exchanges:
4 meat

*To balance your meal add: *Spanish Rice,*
*Vegetable Stir-fry, *Strawberry Sorbet*

*Recipe included in this book

Fillet of Fish Almondine
(Microwave)

After a long day, this elegant dish can be made in minutes in the microwave. It's especially appealing when you have company.

1/4 cup slivered almonds
2 tbsp. margarine
1 pound fish fillets
1/2 tsp. salt
1/8 tsp. pepper
1/4 tsp. dill weed
1 tsp. chopped fresh parsley
1 tbsp. lemon juice
Lemon wedges, fresh parsley, paprika for garnish

Place almonds and margarine in microwave-safe baking dish. Cook, covered, on high for 5 minutes until almonds are golden brown. Remove almonds and set aside.

Place fish fillets in baking dish, turning once to coat with margarine. Sprinkle with salt, pepper, dill, parsley, and lemon juice.

Roll fillets and leave in baking dish, seam side down. Cover with waxed paper. Cook on high for 4 minutes.

Sprinkle almonds over fish. Cook, covered, on high for 1 minute or until fish flakes easily with fork. Let stand 4 minutes before serving. Garnish with lemon wedges, fresh parsley and sprinkle of paprika.

Servings: 4 (4 ounces)
190 calories per serving; 23 gm. protein; 2 gm. carbohydrates;
10 gm. fat; 54 mg. cholesterol; 1 gm. fiber; 1 mg. iron;
40 mg. calcium; 412 mg. sodium

Exchanges:
4 meat, 1 1/2 fat

*To balance your meal add: *Zucchini Couscous,
*Apple Fruit Salad, *Vanilla Tea Cookies*

Recipe included in this book

Microwave Fish Fillets with Carrots

*Although flounder is delicious in this recipe,
other fish could also be used.*

4 large carrots, cut into thin strips
2 tbsp. parsley, minced
1 tsp. olive oil
1/8 tsp. salt
1/8 tsp. pepper
4 flounder fillets (4-5 oz. each)
2 tsp. Dijon mustard
1 tsp. honey

Combine carrots, parsley, oil, salt, and pepper in a 7"x 11"x 2" microwave-safe baking dish. Cover with wax paper. Microwave on high for 5 minutes, stirring once.

Place fish fillets on top of carrots in the corners of the dish with the thick parts of the fish toward the outside of the dish. Combine mustard and honey, and spread over fillets. Cover with wax paper. Cook on high for 2 minutes.

Rotate fillets, placing the cooked parts toward the center. Continue cooking on high for 1 to 3 minutes longer (or until fish flakes easily with a fork).

Let stand a few minutes before serving.

Servings: 6 (4 ounces fish; 1/2 cup carrots)
97 calories per serving; 14 gm. protein; 6 gm. carbohydrates;
2 gm. fat; 34 mg. cholesterol; 2 gm. fiber; 1 mg. iron;
29 mg. calcium; 135 mg. sodium

Exchanges:
1 meat, 1/2 vegetable

To balance your meal add: *Chinese Rice, Molded Fruit Salad

*Recipe included in this book

Tuna-Spinach Casserole
(Microwave)

Here's a nutritious and colorful twist to the old favorite tuna casserole. The spinach adds a boost to your vitamin intake, too.

1 pound fresh spinach
4-oz. can sliced mushrooms
2 tbsp. lemon juice
2 tbsp. margarine
1 tbsp. onion, minced
2 tbsp. flour
1/4 tsp. salt
1/8 tsp. pepper
1 egg, beaten
6 1/8-oz. can water-packed tuna, drained
1/2 cup crumbled potato chips

Rinse and clean spinach well. Drain. Break into pieces, removing tough center stems. Place in 2-quart microwave-safe casserole dish. Cook, covered, on high for 3 to 4 minutes until spinach is limp. Drain. Drain mushrooms into measuring cup. Save liquid. Add lemon juice and water to mushroom liquid to measure 1 cup.

Place margarine in 4-cup glass measure. Cook on high for 45 seconds until margarine is melted. Add onion, flour, salt, and pepper, stirring well. Briskly add mushroom liquid, stirring constantly. Cook, uncovered, on medium for 5 minutes or until thick, stirring twice during cooking time. Add egg to hot mixture, stirring well. Add mushrooms.

Place spinach in casserole dish. Add flaked tuna over spinach. Pour sauce with mushrooms over top. Sprinkle with crushed chips.

Cook, uncovered, on high for 4 minutes. Let stand a few minutes before serving.

Servings: 4 (3/4-cup each)
195 calories per serving; 17 gm. protein; 12 gm. carbohydrates; 10 gm. fat; 66 mg. cholesterol; 4 gm. fiber; 4 mg. iron; 132 mg. calcium; 604 mg. sodium

Exchanges:
1/2 bread, 1 meat, 1 1/2 vegetable, 1/2 fat

To balance your meal add: Mixed Fresh Fruit Cubes, Low-fat Milk

Tuna and Egg a la King

2 tbsp. margarine

3 tbsp. flour

1/2 tsp. salt

1 1/2 cups low-fat milk

3 1/2-oz. can water-packed tuna, drained

2 hard cooked eggs, quartered

1 tsp. green pepper, chopped

2 tsp. pimento, chopped

4 slices bread, toasted

In large skillet, melt margarine. Add flour and salt. Blend until bubbly. Gradually add milk, stirring constantly, until mixture thickens. Remove from heat. Add tuna, eggs, green pepper and pimento. Serve on hot toast.

Servings: 4 (1 slice bread; 1/2 cup tuna)
266 calories per serving; 16 gm. protein; 24 gm. carbohydrates;
12 gm. fat; 120 mg. cholesterol; 3 gm. fiber; 2 mg. iron;
153 mg. calcium; 666 mg. sodium

Exchanges:
1 bread, 1 meat, 1/2 milk, 1/2 fat

*To balance your meal add: *Pea Pods and Water Chestnuts,
Fruit Cobbler*

*Recipe included in this book

Tomato Mushroom Frittata
(Baked Omelet)

A great breakfast treat! Or try as a meal or between meal snack.

1 tbsp. onion, minced
1/2 tsp. garlic, minced
1/2 tbsp. margarine
3 eggs, well beaten
8-10 thin slices fresh tomato
8-10 thin slices fresh mushrooms

Preheat oven to 350°. Sauté onion and garlic in margarine. Remove from heat and pour in eggs. Arrange thin slices of tomato around edge of pan and overlap with thin slices of mushrooms. Bake 5 minutes. Turn oven to 400°. Bake 2 to 3 minutes longer.

Servings: 6 (1/2 cup)
60 calories per serving; 4 gm. protein; 3 gm. carbohydrates;
4 gm. fat; 106 mg. cholesterol; 1 gm. fiber; 1 mg. iron;
18 mg. calcium; 47 mg. sodium

Exchanges:
1/2 meat, 1/2 vegetable

*To balance your meal add: *Flower Garden Biscuits,
Canadian Bacon, Melon Balls*

*Recipe included in this book

Tangy Marinated Flank Steak

Plan ahead and prepare this delicious dish for tomorrow's dinner.

1/2 tsp. garlic powder
1/4 cup soy sauce
1/4 cup lime juice
3 tbsp. honey
2 tbsp. oil
3 green onions, cut diagonally
1 pound flank steak, scored

Prepare marinade by combining the first 6 ingredients in a bowl. Pour over flank steak. Let marinate in refrigerator overnight or at least 2 hours. Add additional water to marinade if too sugary or sticky.

When ready to prepare, broil meat approximately 5 to 6 minutes on each side, until cooked throughout.

Servings: 6 (3 ounces)
239 calories per serving; 21 gm. protein; 11 gm. carbohydrates;
12 gm. fat; 51 mg. cholesterol; 0 fiber; 2 mg. iron;
13 mg. calcium; 751 mg. sodium

Exchanges:
3 meat, 1/2 fruit, 1 fat

*To balance your meal add: *Fast Fried Rice,
Steamed Glazed Carrots

Recipe included in this book

Lazy Day Beef Pie

1 1/2 pounds lean stew beef, cut in small pieces
2 tbsp. flour
1/2 tsp. each salt and pepper
1/2 cup onion, chopped
2 cups water
2 cups canned mixed peas and carrots, drained
1 package Jiffy® corn bread mix
Vegetable oil cooking spray

Sprinkle beef with flour, salt, and pepper. Combine beef, onion, and water in saucepan. Cover and simmer for 1 1/2-2 hours.

When meat is tender, add peas and carrots. Transfer to casserole dish sprayed with vegetable oil cooking spray. Top with corn bread mix prepared according to package directions.

Bake at 425° for 20 minutes.

Servings: 8 (3/4 cup each)
224 calories per serving; 19 gm. protein; 13 gm. carbohydrates;
11 gm. fat; 61 mg. cholesterol; 3 gm. fiber; 3 mg. iron;
29 mg. calcium; 411 mg. sodium

Exchanges:
1/2 bread, 2 meat, 1 vegetable, 1 fat

*To balance your meal add: *Oven Fried Vegetables, Low-fat Milk6*

Recipe included in this book

Polynesian Pork Tenderloins

Try this easy, elegant meal for special occasions or just when you want something special for your family.

2 pork tenderloins, approximately 2 1/2 to 3 pounds
salt and pepper
12-oz. jar plum preserves
2 tbsp. lemon juice
2 tbsp. soy sauce

Place tenderloins on rack in roasting pan. Sprinkle with salt and pepper. Roast at 325° for 45 minutes to 1 hour.

Combine remaining ingredients in small saucepan and bring to boil. Drizzle 1/4 of the sauce over roast during the last 15 minutes of roasting. Slice tenderloins and serve with hot plum sauce.

Servings: 8
262 calories per serving; 40 gm. protein; 8 gm. carbohydrates;
7 gm. fat; 112 mg. cholesterol; 0 fiber; 2 mg. iron;
13 mg. calcium; 345 mg. sodium

Exchanges:
4 meat, 1/2 fruit

*To balance your meal add: *Fruited Rice,
Steamed Broccoli, *Chunky Apple Muffin*

*Recipe included in this book

Zucchini Pizza

What a great choice for a light dinner or appetizer!

3 medium zucchini
2 tbsp. oil
3/4 cup marinara (or pizza) sauce
1/2 tsp. basil
1 cup mozzarella cheese, shredded
1/4 cup Parmesan cheese

Preheat oven to 425°. Cut each zucchini into 4 long strips, each approximately 1/4" wide. Brush with oil. Arrange zucchini strips side by side on cookie sheet or pizza pan. Bake 10 minutes until zucchini is tender.

Combine sauce with basil. Spread equally on zucchini strips. Sprinkle with mozzarella and Parmesan cheeses. Bake an additional 5 minutes until browned.

Servings: 6 (1 slice; 1/3 cup)
161 calories per serving; 10 gm. protein; 9 gm. carbohydrates;
10 gm. fat; 13 mg. cholesterol; 2 gm. fiber; 1 mg. iron;
232 mg. calcium; 346 mg. sodium

Exchanges:
1 meat, 1 vegetable, 1 1/2 fat

*To balance your meal add: *Broccoli, Cheese, and Rice,
Banana Pudding*

Recipe included in this book

Quick Vegetable Pizza

*Although this pizza works best with vegetables, it can also be
made with pieces of cooked chicken or other leftovers.*

10-oz. can refrigerated pizza dough
3/4 cup spaghetti sauce
1/4 cup each raw sliced vegetables, such as carrots,
  broccoli, squash, green peppers, and onions
3 tbsp. Parmesan cheese
1/2 cup mozzarella cheese, shredded

Preheat oven to 350°. Spread dough into a thin rectangle over
cookie or baking sheet. Spread thin layer of sauce over dough.
Add toppings of your choice. Sprinkle with Parmesan and mozzarella cheese.

Bake 10 minutes or until bubbly.

Servings: 10 (one 3" by 5" rectangle)
134 calories per serving; 5 gm. protein; 19 gm. carbohydrates;
4 gm. fat; 4 mg. cholesterol; 1 gm. fiber; 1 mg. iron;
76 mg. calcium; 183 mg. sodium

Exchanges:
1 bread, 1/2 meat, 1/2 vegetable, 1/2 fat

To balance your meal add: *Jiffy Fruit Salad, Rainbow Sherbet

*Recipe included in this book

Corn Dog Twists

Children love corn dogs. Here is a variation you can make at home. If your child doesn't like cheese, just leave it out.

11 1/2-oz. can refrigerator corn bread twists
16 low-fat beef weiners
2 tbsp. melted margarine
1 tbsp. Parmesan cheese

Preheat oven to 375°. Unroll corn bread dough into a long roll. Cut into 16 long strips. Wrap each strip around a weiner. Place on ungreased cookie sheet. Brush lightly with melted margarine. Sprinkle Parmesan cheese over each corn dog twist.

Bake 12 to 16 minutes or until dough is light brown.

Servings: 16 (1 twist)
165 calories per serving; 12 gm. protein; 18 gm. carbohydrates;
14 gm. fat; 39 mg. cholesterol; 0 fiber; 1 mg. iron;
53 mg. calcium; 805 mg. sodium

Exchanges:
1 bread, 1 meat, 2 fat

*To balance your meal add: *Spicy Oven Fried Potatoes,
Molded Apple and Cheese Salad

*Recipe included in this book

Go with Ground Beef

(& Turkey)

Hamburger or Turkey Pie

1 pound lean ground beef (or turkey)
1 medium onion, chopped
2 1/2 cups cooked green beans, drained
10 1/2-oz. can condensed tomato soup
Vegetable oil cooking spray
5 medium boiled potatoes
1/2 cup warm low-fat milk
1 egg, beaten
1/2 tsp. salt
1/8 tsp. pepper

Preheat oven to 350°. Brown ground beef and onion in large skillet. Drain off fat. Add green beans and soup. Pour into 1 1/2-quart casserole sprayed with vegetable oil cooking spray. Mash the potatoes. Add milk, egg, salt, and pepper. Spoon potatoes in mounds over beef in casserole. Bake for 25 minutes.

Servings: 6 (3/4 cup):
340 calories per serving; 22 gm. protein; 35 gm. carbohydrates;
13 gm. fat; 93 mg. cholesterol; 3 gm. fiber; 3 mg. iron;
70 mg. calcium; 592 mg. sodium

Exchanges:
1 1/2 bread, 2 1/2 meat, 1 vegetable, 1 fat

*To balance your meal add: Molded Sliced Peaches in
Orange Gelatin, *Vanilla Tea Cookies*

Recipe included in this book

Quick Sloppy Joes

An all-time favorite for kids and parents alike.

1 pound lean ground beef
1 small onion, chopped
1/2 cup green pepper, chopped
3/4 cup barbecue sauce
1/2 cup frozen corn, defrosted
1/4 tsp. salt
1/8 tsp. pepper
6 buns

Brown ground beef, onion, and green pepper in large skillet. Drain off fat. Add barbecue sauce, corn, salt, and pepper and heat thoroughly. Simmer 5 to 10 minutes. Serve sloppy joes on buns.

Servings: 6 (1/2 cup per bun)
342 calories per serving; 22 gm. protein; 32 gm. carbohydrates;
13 gm. fat; 56 mg. cholesterol; 2 gm. fiber; 3 mg. iron;
82 mg. calcium; 637 mg. sodium

Exchanges:
1 1/2 bread, 2 1/2 meat, 1 vegetable, 1 fat

*To balance your meal add: Mixed Green Salad
with Dressing, *Apple Pudding*

*Recipe included in this book

Indian Corn Stew

*Plan a "Native American" night, and your little
ones will surely enjoy this stew.*

1 pound lean ground beef
1 medium onion, chopped
1/3 cup green pepper, chopped
3 cups corn, fresh or frozen
10 1/2-oz. can condensed tomato soup
2 tsp. sugar
1 tsp. salt
1 tbsp. Worcestershire sauce

Brown ground beef, onion and green pepper in large skillet, stirring frequently. Add corn, tomato soup, sugar, salt, and
Worcestershire sauce. Simmer for 25 minutes.

Servings: 6 (2/3 cup each)
284 calories per serving; 20 gm. protein; 28 gm. carbohydrates;
11 gm. fat; 56 mg. cholesterol; 3 gm. fiber; 3 mg. iron;
23 mg. calcium; 773 mg. sodium

Exchanges:
1 bread, 2 1/2 meat, 1 vegetable, 1 fat

To balance your meal add: Baked Potato, Fresh Fruit Cup

Chili and Corn

*Why not try some corn bread with this chili
for an all-American meal?*

1 pound lean ground beef (or turkey)
1 medium onion, chopped
3 tbsp. chili powder
2 tsp. cumin
1/2 tsp. garlic powder
1 tsp. salt
1/8 tsp. Tabasco® sauce
16-oz. can chopped tomatoes, undrained
2 cups frozen whole kernel corn

Brown ground beef and onion in large skillet. Drain off fat. Stir in
seasonings. Add tomatoes and corn. Bring to boil. Reduce heat
and simmer 20 minutes before serving.

Servings: 6 (3/4 cup each)
250 calories per serving; 20 gm. protein; 19 gm. carbohydrates;
11 gm. fat; 56 mg. cholesterol; 4 gm. fiber; 3 mg. iron;
50 mg. calcium; 562 mg. sodium

Exchanges:
1/2 bread, 2 1/2 meat, 1 1/2 vegetable, 1 fat

*To balance your meal add: Cornbread Sticks,
Chewy Chocolate Brownies

*Recipe included in this book

77

South of the Border Hash

1 pound ground beef
1 small onion, chopped
3 cups frozen O'Brien potatoes, defrosted
1/2 tsp. salt
1/4 tsp. pepper
1 tsp. chili powder
1 cup salsa
6 ripe olives, sliced

Brown ground beef and onion in large skillet. Drain off fat. Stir in potatoes, salt, pepper, and chili powder. Cook over high heat for 5 minutes, stirring occasionally.

Stir salsa into mixture. Cook an additional 10 minutes or until potatoes are lightly browned. Serve in bowl and garnish with sliced olives.

Servings: 8 (1 cup each)
201 calories per serving; 15 gm. protein; 15 gm. carbohydrates;
9 gm. fat; 45 mg. cholesterol; 2 gm. fiber; 2 mg. iron;
43 mg. calcium; 464 mg. sodium

Exchanges:
1/2 bread, 2 meat, 1/2 vegetable, 1 fat

To balance your meal add: Steamed Peapods,
*Ice Cream Fruit Salad

*Recipe included in this book

Taco Balls

*If your children love tacos, here's a switch they are
sure to love as well. For a less spicy taste, cut back on the amount
of taco seasoning you include.*

1 pound lean ground beef
1 1/4-oz. package taco seasoning mix
1/2-3/4 cup water
1 cup cheddar cheese, shredded
3 cups dry biscuit mix (low-fat mix works, and has less
    fat and fewer calories)

Preheat oven to 350°. Combine all ingredients together in large
bowl. (Do not cook ground beef.) Shape mixture into small balls.
Bake on ungreased cookie sheet for 15 to 20 minutes or until
browned.

Servings: 40 balls (1 ball each)
62 calories per serving; 4 gm. protein; 4 gm. carbohydrates;
4 gm. fat; 10 mg. cholesterol; 0 fiber; 1 mg. iron;
34 mg. calcium; 62 mg. sodium

Exchanges:
1/2 bread, 1/2 meat, 1/2 fat

*To balance your meal add: *Salsa, *Spanish Rice, Fruit Cocktail*

*Recipe included in this book

Taco Pie

If your kids like tacos, they're sure to love this all-in-one pie.

1 pound lean ground beef
1 medium onion, chopped
1 1/4-oz. package taco seasoning mix
3/4 cup water
16-oz. jar refried beans
1/3 cup salsa
1 baked 9-inch pastry shell
1/2 cup taco chips, crushed
1/4 cup cheddar cheese, shredded
Shredded lettuce, chopped tomatoes, as desired

Preheat oven to 400°. Brown ground beef and onion in large skillet. Drain off fat. Add taco seasoning mix and water, stirring well. Bring mixture to boil. Reduce heat and simmer 15 minutes.

Combine beans and salsa. Spoon half of the bean mixture into bottom of pastry shell. Top with half of the meat mixture and taco chips. Repeat layers with bean and meat mixtures and top with shredded cheese.

Bake for 20 minutes. Top with lettuce, tomatoes, and additional salsa, if desired.

Servings: 10 (1/10 pie)
271 calories per serving; 15 gm. protein; 21 gm. carbohydrates;
14 gm. fat; 37 mg. cholesterol; 4 gm. fiber; 2 mg. iron;
64 mg. calcium; 419 mg. sodium

Exchanges:
1 bread, 2 meat, 1/2 vegetable, 1 1/2 fat

To balance your meal add: Fruit Cup,
*Chewy Oatmeal Chocolate Cookies

*Recipe included in this book

Porcupine Meatballs

10 3/4-oz. can tomato soup
1 pound lean ground beef (or turkey)
1/4 cup long grain rice, uncooked
1 egg, slightly beaten
1/4 cup onion, chopped
2 tbsp. parsley, chopped
1 tsp. salt
1 tbsp. margarine
1 small clove garlic, minced
1 cup water

Combine 1/4 of the soup and all of the beef, rice, egg, onion, parsley, and salt in large bowl. Shape into 12 balls about 2" in diameter. Melt margarine in large skillet. Add minced garlic. Brown meatballs in skillet. Drain excess fat. Combine remaining soup and water. Pour over browned meatballs. Cover and simmer for 30 to 40 minutes until rice is tender.

Servings: 6 (2 meatballs each)
246 calories per serving; 19 gm. protein; 14 gm. carbohydrates;
13 gm. fat; 91 mg. cholesterol; 0 fiber; 3 mg. iron;
22 mg calcium; 789 mg. sodium

Exchanges:
1/2 bread, 2 meat, 1/2 vegetable, 1 fat

*To balance your meal add: *Confetti Corn, *Apple Pudding*

Recipe included in this book

All-American Meatballs
(Microwave)

Try these easy delicious meatballs over rice, pasta or noodles.

1 pound lean ground beef (or turkey)
1 medium potato, peeled and grated
2 tbsp. dried onion soup mix
1 tbsp. dried parsley flakes
1 egg, beaten
2 cups beef broth
1 tbsp. Worcestershire sauce
2 tbsp. cornstarch
2 tbsp. water

Combine ground beef, potatoes, onion soup mix, parsley, and egg in large mixing bowl. Shape into 12 meatballs about 2" in diameter. Set aside.

In a 2-quart microwave-safe casserole dish, combine beef broth and Worcestershire sauce. Add meatballs to sauce. Cook, covered on medium-high for 12 minutes.

Combine cornstarch and water in small bowl. Mix until smooth. Add to meatballs. Cover and cook on medium-high for 4 minutes or until sauce is thickened.

Let stand 5 minutes before serving.

Servings: 6 (2 meatballs)
213 calories per serving; protein; 19 gm.; 8 gm. carbohydrates;
11 gm. fat; 91 mg. cholesterol; 0 fiber; 2 mg. iron;
17 mg. calcium; 500 mg. sodium

Exchanges:
1/2 bread, 2 1/2 meat, 1 fat

To balance your meal add: Buttered Noodles,
Seasoned Green Beans, Pear Halves

Western Beef Casserole

Vegetables, pasta, hamburger and cheese—
this one-dish meal contributes to your whole pyramid.

1 pound lean ground beef (or turkey)

1 onion, chopped

1/2 green pepper, chopped

6-oz. can tomato sauce

6-oz. can tomato paste

1 cup water

2 cups noodles, cooked

8-oz. can nibblet corn, drained

1/2 cup Parmesan cheese

Brown beef in large skillet. Remove beef from skillet and drain fat.

Sauté onion and green pepper until tender. Add tomato sauce, paste and water. Bring to boil. Add meat. Simmer 20 minutes. Prepare noodles according to package directions.

Layer half of the noodles, half of the meat and half of the corn in casserole dish. Repeat layers. Top with Parmesan cheese.

Servings: 8 (1/2 cup)
262 calories per serving; 19 gm. protein; 23 gm. carbohydrates;
11 gm. fat; 60 mg. cholesterol; 3 gm. fiber; 3 mg. iron;
112 mg. calcium; 538 mg. sodium

Exchanges:
1 bread, 2 meat, 1 vegetable, 1 fat

To balance your meal add: Waldorf Salad,
*Peanut Butter Oatmeal Cookies

*Recipe included in this book

Quick Chili Con Carne
(Microwave)

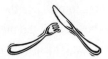

1 pound lean ground beef
1/4 cup onion, chopped
3/4 cup green pepper, chopped
1 clove garlic, minced
2 tbsp. chili powder
1 tsp. salt
16-oz. can chopped tomatoes, undrained
16-oz. can kidney or red beans, undrained

Crumble ground beef into 2-quart microwave-safe casserole dish. Add onion, green pepper, and garlic. Cook, uncovered, on high for 4 minutes. Drain off fat. Add chili powder, salt, undrained tomatoes, and beans. Cook, covered, on medium-high for 15-18 minutes, stirring once after 8 minutes. Let stand 5 minutes before serving.

Servings: 6 (1 cup)
259 calories per serving; 22 gm. protein; 18 gm. carbohydrates; 11 gm. fat; 56 mg. cholesterol; 7 gm. fiber; 3 mg. iron; 55 mg. calcium; 802 mg. sodium

Exchanges:
1 bread, 2 1/2 meat, 1 vegetable, 1 fat

*To balance your meal add: *Broccoli Cornbread, Molded Salad with Banana Slices*

Recipe included in this book

Macaroni and Chili

1 pound lean ground beef (or turkey)
1/2 cup chopped onions
1 tbsp. chili powder
16-oz. can chopped tomatoes, undrained
8-oz. can red kidney beans, undrained
2 cloves garlic, minced
4 dashes Tabasco® sauce, optional
4 cups cooked macaroni noodles, prepared per package

Brown beef in large skillet. Drain off fat. Add onions and chili powder. Cook until meat is no longer pink and onion is tender.

Add undrained tomatoes, undrained kidney beans, garlic, and Tabasco® sauce, if desired. Bring to boil. Reduce heat and simmer, uncovered, for 5 minutes, stirring occasionally.

Add cooked macaroni to chili. Stir together. Serve hot.

Servings: 6 (1 cup each)
339 calories per serving; 24 gm. protein; 38 gm. carbohydrates;
10 gm. fat; 56 mg. cholesterol; 5 gm. fiber; 4 mg. iron;
48 mg. calcium; 313 mg. sodium

Exchanges:
2 bread, 2 meat, 1 vegetable, 1 fat

*To balance your meal add: *Jiffy Fruit Salad, Sherbet*

Recipe included in this book

Tomato Green Chili Tortilla Casserole

Spice up your dinner tonight with this hearty casserole.

1 pound lean ground beef (or turkey)
2 tsp. onion flakes
10 3/4-oz. can cream of mushroom soup
10 3/4-oz. can cream of chicken soup
10-oz. can stewed tomatoes with green chili
6 corn tortillas
Vegetable oil cooking spray
1/2 cup cheddar cheese, shredded

Preheat oven to 375°. Brown ground beef and onion flakes together. Drain off fat. Stir in both soups and canned tomatoes. Cut or tear tortillas into bite-sized pieces. Spray casserole dish with vegetable oil cooking spray. Layer tortilla pieces with meat mixture. Sprinkle cheese over top. Bake 30 minutes.

Servings: 10 (1/2 cup each)
146 calories per serving; 12 gm. protein; 11 gm. carbohydrates;
6 gm. fat; 31 mg. cholesterol; 1 gm. fiber; 1 mg. iron;
75 mg. calcium; 373 mg. sodium

Exchanges:
1 bread, 1 meat, 1/2 vegetable, 1 fat

*To balance your meal add: Mixed Green Salad
with Dressing, *Fruit Ambrosia*

*Recipe included in this book

Turkey Burgers

*A quick alternative to beef hamburgers, and so delicious, too.
Your kids will love them.*

1/4 cup green onion, sliced
1/4 cup carrot, shredded
1 clove garlic, minced
1 pound ground turkey
1 egg
1/3 cup rolled oats
2 tbsp. catsup
1/2 tsp. chili powder
1/4 tsp. paprika
1/4 tsp. pepper
1/2 cup corn flake crumbs

Preheat oven to 400°. Combine onion, carrots and garlic in microwave-safe dish. Cover and cook for 2 minutes until vegetables are tender. Add turkey, egg, oats, catsup, chili powder, paprika, and pepper to vegetables. Mix well.

Shape mixture into patties. Coat each patty with corn flake crumbs. Place patties on baking dish. Cook about 20 to 30 minutes until patties are golden brown and cooked throughout.

Servings: 6 (4 oz. patty)
206 calories per serving; 19 gm. protein; 12 gm. carbohydrates;
9 gm. fat; 93 mg. cholesterol; 1 gm. fiber; 2 mg. iron;
46 mg calcium; 208 mg sodium

Exchanges:
1/2 bread, 2 1/2 meat

*To balance your meal add: *Baked Cranberry and
Apple Casserole, *Homemade Chocolate Pudding*

Beefy Turnovers

A hearty appetizer or smaller meal.

1/2 pound lean ground beef
1/4 cup onion, chopped
1/4 cup green pepper, chopped
1/4 tsp. garlic, minced
8-oz. can tomato sauce
1/3 cup steak sauce
1 cup mozzarella cheese, shredded
2 10-oz. cans refrigerated pizza dough
Vegetable oil cooking spray

Recipe included in this book

Preheat oven to 375°. In large skillet cook ground beef, onion, green pepper, and garlic until meat is brown. Drain off fat. Add sauces. Heat to boiling. Reduce heat. Simmer 5 minutes until thick. Remove from heat. Stir in cheese. Cool 15 minutes.

Unroll pizza dough and cut into 8 equal rectangles. Spoon beef mixture into center of each. Fold into triangles and press edges together with tines of fork. Place on baking sheet that has been sprayed with vegetable oil cooking spray. Bake 20 minutes or until dough is lightly browned.

Servings: 16 (1 turnover each)
184 calories per serving; 8 gm. protein; 19 gm. carbohydrates;
2 gm. fat; 11 mg. cholesterol; 2 gm. fiber; 1 mg. iron;
56 mg. calcium; 368 mg. sodium

Exchanges:
1 bread, 1 meat, 1/2 vegetable, 1/2 fat

*To balance your meal add: *Mixed Vegetable Casserole,
Rainbow Fruit Sticks

*Recipe included in this book

Add Variety with Vegetables

Oven Fried Vegetables

1/4 cup margarine, melted
1 egg
1 tbsp. water
1/2 cup flour
1/2 tsp. salt
1/2 tsp. pepper
3 cups cut up fresh vegetables (broccoli, cauliflower,
    carrots, peppers, mushrooms)

Preheat oven to 400°. Melt margarine in small dish. In another small dish, beat egg and add water. In yet another small dish, mix flour, salt, and pepper.

Dip vegetables pieces in egg mixture, then flour mixture. Place on cookie sheet. Brush with melted margarine. Bake for 7-8 minutes on each side until golden brown.

Servings: 6 (1/2 cup each)
132 calories per serving; 3 gm. protein; 11 gm. carbohydrates;
9 gm. fat; 35 mg. cholesterol; 2 gm. fiber; 1 mg. iron;
23 mg. calcium; 291 mg. sodium

Exchanges:
1/2 bread, 1/2 vegetable

*To balance your meal add: *Oven Poached Fish,
Strawberry Sorbet

*Recipe included in this book

Baked Cranberry and Apple Casserole

When you have more time, try this tasty treat.
It's great for special occasions too.

1 1/2 cups tart apples, peeled and sliced
1 1/2 cups delicious apples, peeled and sliced
2 cups cranberries, washed
1 cup oats
1 cup sugar
1/2 cup brown sugar
1/2 cup chopped pecans, optional
2 tbsp. margarine

Preheat oven to 325°. Layer greased 3-quart casserole dish with both types of apples and cranberries. Combine oats, sugars, and pecans if desired. Pour sugar mixture over apples and cranberries. Dot with margarine. Bake for 1 hour.

Servings: 8 (1/2 cup each)
230 calories per serving; 2 gm. protein; 50 gm. carbohydrates;
4 gm. fat; 0 cholesterol; 3 gm. fiber; 1 mg. iron;
18 mg. calcium; 38 mg. sodium

Exchanges:
1/2 bread, 3 fruit

To balance your meal add: *Tuna Melt Potato

*Recipe included in this book

Mexican Corn Pudding

Want to do something different with canned corn?
Here's just what you are looking for.

16-oz. can cream-style corn
2 eggs, slightly beaten
1/2 cup dry, saltine cracker crumbs
1 tsp. onion, chopped
2 tbsp. green pepper, chopped
2 tbsp. pimento, chopped
1/2 tsp. salt
1/4 tsp. pepper
1/4 tsp. dry mustard
Vegetable oil cooking spray

Preheat oven to 350°. Combine all ingredients in large bowl.
Pour into casserole dish sprayed with vegetable oil cooking spray.
Bake for 1 hour.

Servings: 6 (1/2 cup each)
103 calories per serving; 4 gm. protein; 18 gm. carbohydrates;
3 gm. fat; 71 mg. cholesterol; 1 gm. fiber; 1 mg. iron;
17 mg. calcium; 480 mg. sodium

Exchanges:
1 bread, 1/2 meat

*To balance your meal add: *Nifty Crispy Chicken Drumsticks,*
**Basil Broccoli and Mushrooms, Low-fat Milk*

*Recipe included in this book

96

Salsa

This is as easy as buying it in a jar.

1 cup fresh parsley
1 clove garlic
2 tomatoes
1 onion
1 green pepper
1/4 tsp. pepper
1/8 tsp. cumin
1/8 tsp. chili powder
1-2 drops hot pepper sauce

Drop parsley and garlic into food processor. Chop well. Add remaining ingredients. Chop in food processor until vegetables are somewhat chunky.

Servings: 24 (1 tablespoon)
7 calories per serving; 0 protein; 1 gm. carbohydrates;
0 fat; 0 cholesterol; 0 fiber; 0 iron;
6 mg. calcium; 3 mg. sodium

Exchanges:
Free

*To balance your meal add: *Taco Pie,
Chilled Pineapple Slices*

Recipe included in this book

Pesto Sauce

This is a wonderful way to use home grown basil from your garden.

1 1/2 cups grated Parmesan cheese
2 cups fresh basil leaves
2 cloves garlic
1 oz. pine nuts
1/4 tsp. pepper
1/2 cup vegetable oil

Combine all ingredients except oil in food processor and blend. Slowly dribble oil into food processor while running. Blend until smooth and mixed well. Serve over hot pasta.

Servings: 12 (2 tablespoons)
152 calories per serving; 6 gm. protein; 1 gm. carbohydrates;
14 gm. fat; 10 mg. cholesterol; 0 fiber; 1 mg. iron;
184 mg. calcium; 233 mg. sodium

Exchanges:
1 meat, 2 fat

*To balance your meal add: Plain Noodles,
Tossed Green Salad, *No-Cook Applesauce*

Recipe included in this book

Oriental Spinach

An oriental meal can be made extravagant by adding this easy dish. And, spinach is loaded with vitamin A and beta carotene, too!

1 pound fresh spinach
1 tbsp. vegetable oil
8 large mushrooms, sliced
1/4 cup chicken broth
8 oz. bamboo shoots

Tear spinach into bite-sized pieces. Stir-fry spinach in oil for 2 minutes. Add remaining ingredients. Stir-fry until heated through.

Servings: 4 (1/2 cup each)
77 calories per serving; 5 gm. protein; 7 gm. carbohydrates;
4 gm. fat; 0 cholesterol; 4 gm. fiber; 4 mg. iron;
119 mg. calcium; 143 mg. sodium

Exchanges:
2 vegetables, 1/2 fat

*To balance your meal add: *Porcupine Meatballs,
Warmed Dinner Rolls, *Homemade Chocolate Pudding*

*Recipe included in this book

Pea Pods and Water Chestnuts

1 tbsp. vegetable oil
1 tbsp. green onion, chopped
1 clove garlic, minced
1/2 pound fresh pea pods
1/2 cup water chestnuts, sliced
1 tbsp. soy sauce
1/4 cup chicken broth
1 tsp. cornstarch
1 tbsp. water

Heat oil in skillet. Sauté onion and garlic. Add pea pods, water chestnuts, and soy sauce. Cook 1 minute. Add broth. Cover and simmer 5 minutes.

Combine cornstarch and water. Add to skillet. Cook for 1 minute until sauce thickens.

Servings: 4 (1/2 cup each)
72 calories per serving; 2 gm. protein; 8 gm. carbohydrates;
4 gm. fat; 0 cholesterol; 2 gm. fiber; 1 mg. iron;
20 mg. calcium; 309 mg. sodium

Exchanges:
1 vegetable, 1/2 fat

*To balance your meal add: *Microwave Fish Fillets with Carrots, Warm Dinner Rolls, Fresh Sliced Apple*

Recipe included in this book

Basil Broccoli and Mushrooms

Jazz up your traditional broccoli with mushrooms.
Kids really enjoy them.

10-oz. package frozen broccoli spears
1 tbsp. margarine
4 1/2-oz. can or jar whole mushrooms, drained
1 1/2 tsp. crushed dry basil

Cook broccoli according to package directions. Drain. Melt margarine in small saucepan. Add mushrooms and basil. Cook 2-3 minutes until mushrooms are heated through.

Place broccoli on serving platter or dish. Spoon mushrooms over. Serve immediately.

Servings: 6 (1/2 cup each)
36 calories per serving; 2 gm. protein; 4 gm. carbohydrates;
2 gm. fat; 0 cholesterol; 2 gm. fiber; 1 mg. iron;
35 mg. calcium; 124 mg. sodium

Exchanges:
1 vegetable

*To balance your meal add: *Chicken Rice a Roni,*
**Raisin Bran Muffins*

Recipe included in this book

Cinnamon Carrots

If you don't like cooked carrots now, you will after you try this recipe. Your family may even fight over them.

2 tbsp. margarine
1 1/2 pounds carrots, peeled and sliced
1/2 tsp. salt
2 tsp. sugar
1/2 tsp. cinnamon

In medium saucepan, melt margarine. Add carrots, salt, sugar, and enough water to barely cover the carrots. Cover and cook on medium-high until carrots are tender, about 15-20 minutes. Remove lid and continue cooking until all water evaporates. Mix in cinnamon.

Servings: 6 (1 / 2 cup each)
89 calories per serving; 1 gm. protein; 13 gm. carbohydrates;
4 gm. fat; 0 cholesterol; 4 gm. fiber; 1 mg. iron;
34 mg. calcium; 262 mg. sodium

Exchanges:
1 1/2 vegetable

To balance your meal add: *Turkey Burgers,
Frozen Yogurt

*Recipe included in this book

Garlic Green Beans

*If you're a family of garlic lovers, you can't
beat this delicious twist to green beans.
Let your children pop the beans for added fun.*

2 pounds fresh green beans
1/3 cup chicken broth
1 tbsp. vegetable oil
4 cloves garlic, crushed
1/4 tsp. pepper

Wash and trim green beans. Steam green beans until barely tender or drop beans into a large pot of boiling water for 2 minutes. Drain and rinse with cold water.

Combine broth and oil in large saucepan. Place over medium heat until hot. Add garlic. Saute 30 seconds. Add beans and toss well. Cook 8-10 minutes until liquid evaporates, stirring occasionally. Remove from heat. Sprinkle with pepper.

Servings: 6 (1/2 cup each)
72 calories per serving; 3 gm. protein; 12 gm. carbohydrates;
3 gm. fat; 0 cholesterol; 5 gm. fiber; 2 mg. iron;
60 mg. calcium; 52 mg. sodium

Exchanges:
1 vegetable, 1/2 fat

*To balance your meal add: *Golden Baked Chicken,
Buttered Pasta, *Quick and Easy Carrot Cake*

Recipe included in this book

Sweetened Glazed Carrots

*Sweeten your cooked carrots and watch your
kid's faces light up with joy.*

3 cups carrots, thinly sliced
1 tbsp. brown sugar
1/2 tsp. dry mustard
1 tbsp. margarine
1/4 tsp. salt

In medium saucepan, cook carrots in small amount of water for
5-8 minutes, until tender-crisp. Drain.

In small saucepan, combine brown sugar, mustard, margarine
and salt. Cook over medium heat until margarine melts, while
stirring constantly. Pour glaze over carrots. Toss gently.

Servings: 6 (1/2 cup each)
57 calories per serving; 1 gm. protein; 10 gm. carbohydrates;
2 gm. fat; 0 cholesterol; 2 gm. fiber; 1 mg. iron;
26 mg. calcium; 158 mg. sodium

Exchanges:
1 vegetable, 1/2 fat

*To balance your meal add: *Fillet of Fish Almondine,
Jiffy Fruit Salad

Recipe included in this book

Confetti Corn

Add a little color to ordinary corn with this small touch.
It's more appealing and tastier, too.

2 tbsp. margarine
2 tbsp. green pepper, chopped
2 tbsp. onion, chopped
10-oz. package frozen corn
1/2 tsp. salt

In large skillet, heat margarine. Add green pepper and onion. Sauté until tender. Add corn and salt. Cover and cook over medium heat until corn is tender, about 5 minutes, stirring occasionally.

Servings: 4 (1/2 cup each)
111 calories per serving; 2 gm. protein; 15 gm. carbohydrates;
6 gm. fat; 0 cholesterol; 2 gm. fiber; 0 iron;
5 mg. calcium; 323 mg. sodium

Exchanges:
1 bread, 1 fat

To balance your meal add: Grilled Hamburger on Bun,
Fresh Fruit Cup

Mixed Vegetable Casserole

*Other vegetables may be substituted for any
of the vegetables in this casserole.*

10-oz. package frozen carrots
10-oz. package frozen broccoli
10-oz. package frozen cauliflower
10 3/4-oz. can cream of mushroom soup
1/2 8-oz. jar Cheez Whiz®
1 cup crisp chow mein noodles

Preheat oven to 375°.

Cook all vegetables 1/2 of the cooking time stated on packages. Place vegetables in large casserole dish. In saucepan, blend and heat soup and Cheez Whiz. Pour over top of vegetables and mix carefully. Bake 25-30 minutes. Top with chow mein noodles during the last 5 minutes of baking.

Servings: 16 (1/3 cup each)
104 calories per serving; 5 gm. protein; 10 gm. carbohydrates;
6 gm. fat; 8 mg. cholesterol; 3 gm. fiber; 1 mg. iron;
77 mg. calcium; 380 mg. sodium

Exchanges:
1/2 bread, 1 vegetable, 1 fat

*To balance your meal add: *Corn Dog Twist,
Rainbow Fruit Sticks

Recipe included in this book

Lima Beans in Sour Cream

Beans are a wonderful source of fiber.
Why not try them more often?

2 10-oz. packages frozen baby lima beans
1 medium onion, chopped
1 cup low-fat sour cream
2-oz. jar pimentos, chopped
1 tbsp. flour
1/2 tsp. salt
Black pepper, to taste

Combine lima beans and onions in medium saucepan. Cook according to package directions. Add sour cream and remaining ingredients. Heat thoroughly over low heat for 8 minutes.

Servings: 8 (1/2 cup each)
128 calories per serving; 6 gm. protein; 18 gm. carbohydrates;
4 gm. fat; 12 mg. cholesterol; 5 gm. fiber; 2 mg. iron;
56 mg. calcium; 168 mg. sodium

Exchanges:
1 bread, 1/2 vegetable, 1/2 fat

*To balance your meal add: *Tomato Mushroom Frittata,*
**Apple Juice Biscuit*

Recipe included in this book

Grab a Grain

Fruited Rice

2 cups chicken broth
1 cup long grain rice
2 1/2-oz. jar sliced mushrooms
1/3 cup onion, chopped
2 tbsp. margarine
8 3/4-oz. can pineapple chunks, drained
2 tbsp. diced pimentos
1 1/2 tbsp. soy sauce
1/4 tsp. salt
dash pepper

Heat chicken broth in medium saucepan to boiling. Add rice. Cover and simmer until liquid is absorbed, about 25 minutes.

Sauté mushrooms and onion in margarine. Add pineapple and pimentos. Combine rice with mushroom and onion mixture. Stir in soy sauce, salt, and pepper.

Servings: 8 (1/2 cup each)
145 calories per serving; 3 gm. protein; 25 gm. carbohydrates;
3 gm. fat; 0 cholesterol; 1 gm. fiber; 1 mg. iron;
17 mg. calcium; 526 mg. sodium

Exchanges:
1 bread

*To balance your meal add: *Parmesan Chicken Nuggets,
Steamed Green Beans, Low-fat Milk*

*Recipe included in this book

Fast Fried Rice
(Microwave)

*Whoever thought fried rice could be made this easily.
It's delicious and microwaved, not fried.*

1 1/2 cups uncooked instant rice
1 1/2 cups hot tap water
3/4 cup shredded carrots (about 2)
1/4 cup green onion, chopped
2 tbsp. soy sauce
2 tsp. margarine
1/2 tsp. garlic powder

Combine all ingredients in 2-quart casserole dish. Cover and microwave on medium-high for 6-8 minutes until rice is tender and water is absorbed. Remove from microwave. Let stand, covered, 5-7 minutes. Fluff with a fork before serving.

Servings: 6 (3/4 cup each)
117 calories per serving; 3 gm. protein; 23 gm. carbohydrates;
1 gm. fat; 0 cholesterol; 1 gm. fiber; 1 mg. iron;
15 mg. calcium; 365 mg. sodium

Exchanges:
1 bread, 1/2 vegetable, 1/2 fat

*To balance your meal add: *Shrimp and Pepper Stir-Fry,
Chewy Oatmeal Chocolate Cookies

*Recipe included in this book

Spanish Rice

The zesty taste of this dish appeals to old and young alike.

2 1/2 cups cooked rice
3 strips bacon, cooked crisp, crumbled
3 tbsp. onion, chopped
1/4 cup green pepper, chopped
16-oz. can chopped tomatoes
1 tbsp. sugar
1 tsp. salt
1/4 tsp. pepper

Preheat oven to 350°. Prepare rice according to package directions. Prepare bacon. Remove bacon from skillet. Add onion and green pepper. Sauté until onion is tender. Add tomatoes, sugar, salt, pepper, and cooked rice.

Pour mixture into casserole dish. Bake 25-30 minutes.

Servings: 8 (1/2 cup each)
84 calories per serving; 2 gm. protein; 15 gm. carbohydrates;
1 gm. fat; 2 mg. cholesterol; 1 gm. fiber; 1 mg. iron;
21 mg. calcium; 398 mg. sodium

Exchanges:
1/2 bread, 1/2 vegetable

*To balance your meal add: *Golden Baked Fish Fillet,
Fruit Ambrosia

Recipe included in this book

Chinese Rice

Any plain meal can be special with the added touch of this rice dish.

2 tbsp. margarine
2 eggs, lightly beaten
3 cups cooked rice
1/2 onion, sliced
1 tsp. salt
1/4 tsp. pepper
16-oz. can bean sprouts, drained
1/3 cup fresh green onion tops, optional

In a large skillet or wok, melt margarine. Add eggs. Stir-fry several minutes on each side until done but not too firm. Break up with fork while cooking. Add rice, onion, salt, pepper, bean sprouts, and green onion, if desired. Cook on medium heat about 10 minutes until heated through, covering pan during last 2 minutes.

Serve on large platter or form into a large greased mold.

Servings: 8 (1/2 cup each)
154 calories per serving; 5 gm. protein; 24 gm. carbohydrates;
4 gm. fat; 53 mg. cholesterol; 1 gm. fiber; 1 mg. iron;
25 mg. calcium; 396 mg. sodium

Exchanges:
1 bread, 1/2 vegetable

To balance your meal add: *All-American Meatballs,
*Oriental Spinach
*Recipe included in this book

Easy Rice Souffle

1 tbsp. margarine
1 tbsp. flour
1 cup low-fat milk
2 eggs, separated
2 cups cooked rice
3/4 cup cheddar cheese, shredded
1/4 tsp. onion juice (or 1 tbsp. chopped onion
    pressed in garlic press)
Salt and pepper to taste
Vegetable oil cooking spray

Preheat oven to 350°. Melt margarine in saucepan. Stir in flour
and milk until mixture is smooth. Cool slightly. Add egg yolks,
rice, cheese, onion juice, salt, and pepper.

   Beat egg whites until stiff. Fold into mixture. Pour into casserole
dish sprayed with vegetable oil cooking spray. Bake for 20 minutes.

Servings: 6 (1/2 cup each)
213 calories per serving; 9 gm. protein; 23 gm. carbohydrates;
9 gm. fat; 89 mg. cholesterol; 0 fiber; 1 mg. iron;
167 mg. calcium; 152 mg. sodium

Exchanges:
1 bread, 1 meat, 1 fat

To balance your meal add: *Tossed Salad Pita,
*Peanut Butter Pudding

*Recipe included in this book

Broccoli, Cheese, and Rice
(Microwave)

A hot side dish you can make in minutes.
Kids (both young and old) love it.

10-oz. package frozen chopped broccoli
2 cups instant rice (white or brown), uncooked
1/2 8-oz. jar Cheez Whiz®

Cook broccoli in microwave according to package directions. Cook rice in microwave according to package directions. Drain broccoli and mix with cooked rice. Add Cheez Whiz and mix thoroughly. Serve immediately.

Servings: 12 (1/2 cup each)
105 calories per serving; 4 gm. protein; 17 gm. carbohydrates;
3 gm. fat; 6 mg. cholesterol; 0 fiber; 1 mg. iron;
44 mg. calcium; 171 mg. sodium;

Exchanges:
1/2 bread, 1/2 vegetable, 1/2 fat

To balance your meal add: *Homemade Chicken Nuggets,
*No-Cook Applesauce

*Recipe included in this book

Zucchini Couscous
(Microwave)

This Moroccan pasta is fluffy, tasty, and goes great with any meal.

1 medium zucchini, chopped

2 tbsp. green onion, chopped

1 tsp. dried parsley

2 tbsp. soy sauce

2 tbsp. white cooking wine

1/4 tsp. garlic powder

1/2 cup uncooked couscous

1/2 cup water

1 tbsp. margarine

In 2-quart microwave-safe baking dish, combine zucchini, onion, parsley, soy sauce, wine, and garlic powder. Cover and microwave on medium high for 2 minutes. Add remaining ingredients. Cook for 3 minutes longer. Remove from microwave. Let stand 5 minutes before serving.

Servings: 4 (1/2 cup each)

128 calories per serving; 3 gm. protein; 21 gm. carbohydrates;
3 gm. fat; 0 cholesterol; 1 gm. fiber; 2 mg. iron;
21 mg. calcium; 551 mg. sodium

Exchanges:
1 bread, 1/2 vegetable

*To balance your meal add: *Beefy Turnovers, *Easy Apple Cake*

*Recipe included in this book

Couscous with Vegetables

3 tomatoes, chopped
15-oz. can garbanzo beans, drained
1/2 cup mushrooms, sliced
1/3 cup green onion, chopped
1 tsp. oregano
1 tsp. paprika
1 tsp. parsley
1 tsp. margarine
2 cloves garlic, minced
5 cups cooked couscous, prepared per package
1/4 cup Parmesan cheese

Mix together all ingredients, except couscous and Parmesan cheese, in medium saucepan. Heat thoroughly.

Spoon couscous into serving dish. Top with vegetable mixture. Sprinkle with Parmesan cheese. Serve hot.

Servings: 16 (1/2 cup each)

125 calories per serving; 4 gm. protein; 24 gm. carbohydrates;
1 gm. fat; 1 mg. cholesterol; 2 gm. fiber; 1 mg. iron;
40 mg. calcium; 99 mg. sodium

Exchanges:

1 1/2 bread

*To balance your meal add: *Golden Baked Chicken,*
Gumdrop Bread

*Recipe included in this book

Wrap a Tortilla

tart with a tortilla. Add beans, peppers, corn, tomatoes, squash, olives, rice, beef, pork, chicken, or cheese. Make a taco, fajita, burrito, tostada, enchilada, or tamale. Your choices in Mexican cooking are endless. And best of all, they don't have to be too hot, spicy, or high in fat. It's your chance to create a colorful and exciting meal.

Fun With Tortillas

If you're not clear on what some of these exotic terms mean, these definitions may help.

- **Burrito:** A warm flour tortilla rolled around a mixture of meat, eggs, beans, or avocado. May be eaten for breakfast or as a snack or main dish.

- **Enchilada:** A corn tortilla heated briefly in hot oil, dipped in chili sauce, and wrapped around a filling of cheese, chicken, or beef and onions; served with additional chili sauce.

- **Fajita:** Dish consisting of grilled strips of beef or chicken, often served wrapped in a soft tortilla with vegetable slices or a sauce.

- **Quesadilla:** Flour or corn tortilla folded around sliced or crumbled cheese, then heated to melt the cheese.

- **Taco:** Corn tortillas, lightly fried, folded in half, and fried again until crisp. Tacos usually are filled with seasoned beef, grated cheese, shredded lettuce, and chopped tomatoes. Soft tacos are plain tortillas folded in half around a filling.

- **Tamale:** Spicy meat wrapped in cornmeal or masa, then wrapped in softened corn husks and steamed.

- **Tostada:** Flat fried corn tortilla spread with a thin layer of refried beans, chicken, and guacamole and topped with shredded lettuce, chopped tomato, onion, and grated cheese.

Options for Fillings:

Try some of the recipes that follow or create your own tortilla filling by mixing some of the foods listed here.

Vegetables

beans
peppers
corn
tomatoes
squash
olives
broccoli
mushrooms
cauliflower
peppers
tomatoes
shredded carrots
spinach
onions
shredded lettuce

Grains

rice, white or brown
couscous

Dairy (try low-fat)

cheddar cheese
Mozzarella cheese
sour cream
yogurt
Parmesan cheese
cottage cheese
melted cheese

Meat

pork
shrimp
tuna
beef
diced chicken or turkey
eggs

Sauces

chili
BBQ
salsa

Ground Beef Fajitas

Be creative with fajitas. You can even add extra toppings like chopped tomatoes and low-fat sour cream to fajitas if you want to jazz up your meal.

1 pound lean ground beef
1 onion, sliced
1/2 green pepper, sliced
1/2 red pepper, sliced
1 cup prepared salsa
2 tsp. chili powder
8 flour tortillas

In large nonstick skillet, brown beef, onion, and peppers over medium heat. Drain fat. Stir in salsa and chili powder. Simmer about 5 minutes on low heat, stirring occasionally. Roll beef mixture into tortillas just before serving.

Servings: 4 (2 tortillas)
246 calories per serving; 16 gm. protein; 24 gm. carbohydrates;
9 gm. fat; 42 mg. cholesterol; 2 gm. fiber; 3 mg. iron;
58 mg. calcium; 328 mg. sodium

Exchanges:
1 1/2 bread, 1 1/2 meat, 1/2 vegetable, 1/2 fat

*To balance your meal add: *Italian Vegetable Soup,
Fruity Slurpee

Recipe included in this book

Bean Burrito
(Microwave)

A no-cook meal that's high in fiber and great tasting, too.

4 flour tortillas
2 cups canned black beans
1/2 cup prepared salsa
1/2 cup tomatoes, chopped
2 oz. low-fat cheddar cheese, shredded
1/4 cup low-fat sour cream

Lay tortillas on platter. Fill each equally with beans, salsa, tomatoes, and cheese. Roll up. Microwave about 40 seconds until beans are hot and cheese is melted. Top with sour cream.

Servings: 4 (1 tortilla)
283 calories per serving; 15 gm. protein; 43 gm. carbohydrates;
6 gm. fat; 9 mg. cholesterol; 6 gm. fiber; 3 mg. iron;
187 mg. calcium; 298 mg. sodium

Exchanges:
2 1/2 bread, 1/2 meat, 1/2 vegetable, 1/2 fat

*To balance your meal add: *Bird's Nest Cookies*

*Recipe included in this book

Steak Fajitas

This meal is quick to prepare and satisfying to all ages.

1 tbsp. vegetable oil
1 pound flank steak, cut in thin strips
1 onion, sliced
1 green pepper, sliced
1 red pepper, sliced
1 tsp. garlic powder
1/2 cup water
1/4 cup lime juice
1/4 tsp. pepper
4 tortillas

Heat oil in large skillet or wok. Add steak, vegetables, and garlic powder. Saute until steak is cooked through and vegetables are tender. Add remaining ingredients, except tortillas. Bring to boil. Reduce heat and simmer for 5 minutes. Wrap in a warmed tortilla.

Servings: 6 (1 tortilla)
234 calories per serving; 18 gm. protein; 18 gm. carbohydrates;
10 gm. fat; 38 mg. cholesterol; 2 gm. fiber; 2 mg. iron;
43 mg. calcium; 163 mg. sodium

Exchanges:
1 bread, 2 meat, 1 vegetable, 1 fat

*To balance your meal add: *Salsa, Fresh Apple Slices*

*Recipe included in this book

Chicken Tostadas

*Start with a warm tortilla, mound high with chicken, cheese,
and colorful vegetables, and enjoy. A real treat
for kids and parents alike.*

8 8-inch tortillas
2 chicken breasts, boneless, skinless,
    sliced into thin strips
1/4 cup green onion, sliced
1 tbsp. vegetable oil
8-oz. can tomato sauce
1/2 tsp. garlic powder
1/2 tsp. salt
1/4 tsp. ground cumin
2 cups shredded lettuce
3/4 cup shredded cheese (cheddar, mozzarella,
    or combination)
16 sliced, pitted, ripe olives
Salsa, optional

Heat tortillas briefly in warm oven until ready to serve.

In large skillet over medium-high heat, sauté chicken strips and onion in oil until chicken is no longer pink. Add tomato sauce, garlic powder, salt, and cumin. Reduce heat and simmer 20 minutes.

To assemble tostada, place a warm tortilla on serving plate, spoon on chicken mixture, then lettuce, cheese, and olives. Top with salsa, if desired.

Servings: 8
227 calories per serving; 13 gm. protein; 23 gm. carbohydrates;
9 gm. fat; 28 mg. cholesterol; 2 gm. fiber; 2 mg. iron;
141 mg. calcium; 619 mg. sodium

Exchanges:
1 1/2 bread, 1 meat, 1/2 vegetable, 1 fat

*To balance your meal add: *Salsa, *Strawberry Sorbet*

Recipe included in this book

Quick Quesadillas
(Microwave)

A great after-school snack for hungry kids!

8 8-inch tortillas
1/2 cup refried beans
3/4 cup shredded cheese (any variety)
Salsa, optional

Place 1 tablespoon of beans on each tortilla. Top with shredded cheese. Fold tortilla in half. Microwave on high for 15-20 seconds until cheese is melted. Serve with salsa, if desired.

Servings: 8
174 calories per serving; 7 gm. protein; 29 gm. carbohydrates;
6 gm. fat; 11 mg. cholesterol; 2 gm. fiber; 1 mg. iron;
128 mg. calcium; 302 mg. sodium.

Exchanges:
1 1/2 bread, 1/2 meat, 1 fat

*To balance your meal add: Baby Carrot Sticks, *Salsa,
Homemade Chocolate Pudding

*Recipe included in this book

Peanut Butter and More Fajita

Try this treat for a snack or as part of a quick meal.
Let your kids create their own.

2 tbsp. peanut butter
2 tbsp. applesauce or other filling (chopped apples,
    shredded carrots, shredded zucchini, mashed
    banana, fruit spread)
1 8-inch tortilla
Shredded lettuce, optional

Combine peanut butter with applesauce or other filling of choice.
Place filling in tortilla. Add lettuce, if desired. Roll up tortilla. Eat
immediately.

Servings: 1
316 calories per serving; 11 gm. protein; 30 gm. carbohydrates;
18 gm. fat; 0 cholesterol; 3 gm. fiber; 2 mg. iron;
56 mg. calcium; 322 mg. sodium

Exchanges:
1 1/2 bread, 1 meat, 1 fruit, 2 1/2 fat

To balance your meal add: Celery Sticks and Fresh Pepper Slices,
Low-fat Milk

Pick

a

Potato

A stuffed baked potato has been a popular fast food for years. Adults love them. Kids love them. They are nutritious, delicious, and easy to prepare. Making your own creation from a variety of toppings is a wonderful way to throw together a quick meal. Experiment with various options. Set up a potato bar. Let everyone dive in and create their favorite potato.

Bake the Perfect Potato

- Wash, dry, and then pierce the skin of your potato with a fork. This will allow for the steam to escape while it is cooking.

- Avoid wrapping your potato in foil as this will hold in the steam, thus creating a soggier potato.

- Cook your potato as follows:

  Convection oven—375° for 30-45 minutes
  Conventional oven—425° for 45-60 minutes
  Microwave oven—high power for 5-6 minutes

Cooking times may vary based on the size of the potato and the number of potatoes you are baking.

Options for Toppings:

Try some of our recipes that follow or create your own potato by mixing up some of the toppings suggested here.

Vegetables

broccoli
mushrooms
cauliflower
peppers
tomatoes
shredded carrots
spinach

Dairy (try low-fat)

cheddar cheese
mozzarella cheese
sour cream
yogurt
Parmesan cheese
cottage cheese
melted cheese

Meat

shrimp
tuna
taco beef
diced chicken

Sauces

marinara
chili
BBQ
salsa

Pizza Potato
(Microwave)

If your children are always asking for pizza, try these.

2 baked potatoes
1/4 cup marinara or pizza sauce
1/4 cup green pepper, chopped
1/4 cup mushrooms, chopped
1/4 cup mozzarella cheese, shredded
2 tbsp. Parmesan cheese

Bake potatoes, and cut open. Spoon half of marinara sauce, green pepper and mushrooms into each potato. Heat 1 to 1 1/2 minutes in microwave until vegetables soften. Top with mozzarella cheese. Heat 30 seconds to 1 minute longer until cheese melts. Sprinkle with Parmesan cheese.

Servings: 2 (1 potato)
317 calories per serving; 12 gm. protein; 56 gm. carbohydrates;
6 gm. fat; 12 mg. cholesterol; 5 gm. fiber; 3 mg. iron;
219 mg. calcium; 372 mg. sodium

Exchanges:
3 bread, 1 meat, 1/2 fat

To balance your meal add: *Rainbow Fruit Sticks

*Recipe included in this book

Easy Mexican Potato
(Microwave)

*Enjoy this as is or add a little taco cheese, guacamole,
or low-fat sour cream for a zippier taste.*

2 baked potatoes
1/4 cup prepared salsa
5 low-fat tortilla chips, crushed

Bake potatoes, and cut open. Spoon half of salsa into each potato. Heat in microwave for 30 seconds to 1 minute until heated through. Sprinkle with crushed tortilla chips.

Servings: 2 (1 potato)
243 calories per serving; 5 gm. protein; 55 gm. carbohydrates;
1 gm. fat; 0 cholesterol; 5 gm. fiber; 3 mg. iron;
30 mg. calcium; 173 mg. sodium

Exchanges:
3 bread

*To balance your meal add: Fresh Pepper Slices,
Low-fat Milk*

Vegetable Potato Supreme
(Microwave)

You can cover most of the food guide pyramid with this stuffed potato. Nutritious and low-fat, too!

4 baked potatoes
1 cup fresh broccoli flowerets
1/2 cup fresh mushrooms, sliced
1/4 cup green onion, chopped
1/4 cup red pepper, chopped
1/2 cup nonfat plain yogurt
1/4 cup low-fat milk
2 tsp. cornstarch
1 tsp. Dijon mustard
1 tbsp. Parmesan cheese

Bake potatoes. Combine broccoli, mushrooms, onion, and peppers in microwave-safe dish. Add 2 tbsp. water. Cover and cook for 3-5 minutes on high power until vegetables are tender.

Stir together yogurt, milk, cornstarch, and mustard. Add to vegetable mixture. Cook, covered, for 3 minutes on high power until mixture begins to thicken, stirring occasionally.

Cut open potatoes. Spoon vegetable mixture over hot potatoes. Sprinkle with Parmesan cheese. Serve immediately.

Servings: 4 (1 potato)
270 calories per serving; 9 gm. protein; 58 gm. carbohydrates;
1 gm. fat; 3 mg. cholesterol; 5 gm. fiber; 3 mg. iron;
138 mg. calcium; 100 mg. sodium

Exchanges:
3 bread, 1/2 meat, 1/2 milk

To balance your meal add: Orange Juice

Ratatouille Potato
(Microwave)

4 baked potatoes
1 medium eggplant, peeled and chopped
14 1/2-oz. can whole tomatoes
1 green pepper, chopped
1/3 cup onion, chopped
2 tbsp. tomato paste
1/2 tsp. oregano
1/2 tsp. thyme
1/4 tsp. garlic powder
1/4 tsp. pepper
2 tbsp. Parmesan cheese
1/2 cup shredded mozzarella cheese

Bake potatoes. In microwave-safe casserole dish, combine all ingredients, except potatoes and cheeses. Cook, covered, on high for 15 minutes or until eggplant is tender, stirring occasionally.

Cut potatoes open. Add vegetable mixture. Top with cheeses. Return to microwave and cook 2 minutes more, until cheese melts.

Servings: 4 (1 potato)
308 calories per serving; 11 gm. protein; 59 gm. carbohydrates;
4 gm. fat; 11 mg. cholesterol; 8 gm. fiber; 4 mg. iron;
198 mg. calcium; 374 mg. sodium

Exchanges:
3 bread, 1/2 meat, 1 1/2 vegetable, 1/2 fat

To balance your meal add: Chilled Sliced Peaches

Twice Baked Potatoes
(Microwave)

*Try this potato as an accompaniment to a meal
or as a meal by itself. Low-calorie cream cheese can be used in
place of cottage cheese if you choose.*

2 baked potatoes
1/4 cup cottage cheese or low-fat cream cheese
1/4 cup low-fat milk

1 tbsp. margarine
1 tsp. parsley
1/2 tsp. chives
1/4 tsp. garlic powder
1/8 tsp. pepper
paprika, optional

Bake potatoes. Cut potatoes open. Scoop out pulp, leaving 1/4-inch shell. Place potato pulp in mixing bowl.

In food processor or blender, combine cottage cheese and milk. Process until smooth. Add pulp, margarine, parsley, chives, garlic powder, and pepper. Blend until smooth and fluffy.

Spoon mixture into potato shells. Place on microwave-safe baking dish. Cook on high for 1-2 minutes, until heated through.

Sprinkle with paprika, if desired.

Servings: 2 (1 potato each)
295 calories per serving; 9 gm. protein; 51 gm. carbohydrates;
7 gm. fat; 3 mg. cholesterol; 5 gm. fiber; 3 mg. iron;
71 mg. calcium; 87 mg. sodium

Exchanges:
3 bread, 1/2 meat, 1 fat

*To balance your meal add: *Microwave Fish Fillets with Carrots*

Recipe included in this book

Tuna Melt Potato
(Microwave)

Tuna melts are family favorites. Why not try one in a potato?

4 large baked potatoes
4 tsp. soft spread margarine
6 1/8-oz. can water-packed tuna, drained
1/2 cup mozzarella (or cheddar) cheese, shredded

Bake potatoes. Cut potatoes open. Spread 1 tsp. margarine into each hot potato. Divide tuna equally and spoon into potato. Top with shredded cheese. Microwave about 1 minute or heat until cheese is melted. Serve hot.

Servings: 4 (1 potato)
338 calories per serving; 18 gm. protein; 51 gm. carbohydrates;
7 gm. fat; 19 mg. cholesterol; 4 gm. fiber; 3 mg. iron;
129 mg. calcium; 257 mg. sodium

Exchanges:
3 bread, 1 1/2 meat, 1 fat

To balance your meal add: Fresh Pineapple Chunks

Spicy Oven Fried Potatoes

A better choice than frozen french fries. And, great tasting, too!

3 medium potatoes
2 tbsp. margarine
1/4 tsp. dried basil or oregano
1/4 tsp. garlic salt
1/4 tsp. paprika
1/8 tsp. pepper

Preheat broiler. Scrub potatoes and cut into slices or wedges. Melt margarine. Place margarine and spices in large bowl or resealable bag. Coat potatoes with margarine mixture by stirring in bowl or shaking in bag. Place potatoes in single layer on cookie sheet. Broil potatoes about 5-10 minutes on each side until golden brown.

Servings: 4 (1/2 cup each)
217 calories per serving; 4 gm. protein; 38 gm. carbohydrates;
6 gm. fat; 0 cholesterol; 3 gm. fiber; 2 mg. iron;
20 mg. calcium; 131 mg. sodium

Exchanges:
2 bread

*To balance your meal add: *Polynesian Pork Tenderloins,
Apple Fruit Salad

*Recipe included in this book

Hash Brown Potato Casserole

3 tbsp. vegetable oil
2-pound bag frozen hash brown potatoes
1 small onion, chopped
1 green pepper, chopped
Vegetable oil cooking spray
1 cup cubed or canned ham
4 eggs, beaten
1/2 cup cheddar cheese, shredded
1/4 tsp. pepper

Heat oil in large skillet. Sauté hash browns, onion, and green pepper until potatoes start to brown. Spray 13" x 9" baking dish with vegetable oil cooking spray. Spread potato mixture in baking dish and top with ham and beaten eggs. Stir gently to coat. Sprinkle with cheese and pepper. Refrigerate overnight, if planning to serve in morning.

Preheat oven to 375°. Bake, covered with aluminum foil, for 25 minutes. Remove foil and bake 5 minutes longer.

Servings: 16 (1/2 cup each)
153 calories per serving; 6 gm. protein; 21 gm. carbohydrates;
6 gm. fat; 55 mg. cholesterol; 2 gm. fiber; 1 mg. iron;
34 mg. calcium; 167 mg. sodium

Exchanges:
1 bread, 1 meat, 1 fat

To balance your meal add: Tomato Juice

Orange Yams

Impress your family with these sweet potatoes.

4 sweet potatoes
Vegetable oil cooking spray
1 cup orange juice
1 tsp. grated orange rind
1/2 cup sugar
1/2 cup brown sugar
2 tbsp. flour
2 tbsp. margarine
1 tsp. salt

Parboil sweet potatoes. Peel and cut in half. Place in baking dish sprayed with vegetable oil cooking spray. Preheat oven to 350°.

Combine remaining ingredients in saucepan. Bring to boil and simmer for 10 minutes. Pour mixture over potatoes. Bake, uncovered, for 40 minutes.

Servings: 8 (1/2 cup each)
187 calories per serving; 1 gm. protein; 40 gm. carbohydrates; 3 gm. fat;
0 cholesterol; 2 gm. fiber; 1 mg. iron; 29 mg. calcium; 310 mg. sodium

Exchanges:
1 bread, 2 fruit

*To balance your meal add: *Polynesian Pork Tenderloins,
Warmed Dinner Rolls*

*Recipe included in this book

Oven Fried Potato Duet

Jazz up an ordinary potato dish with a combination
of white and sweet potatoes. Not only do they add color to
your plate, but they add more nutrition, too.

Vegetable oil cooking spray
2 baking potatoes
2 sweet potatoes
1/2 tsp. paprika

Preheat oven to 450°. Spray cookie sheet with vegetable oil cooking spray. Cut unpeeled potatoes into thin wedges. Arrange in single layer on cookie sheet. Spray potatoes with vegetable oil cooking spray. Sprinkle with paprika. Bake 20 minutes or until potatoes are golden brown and tender.

Servings: 4 (1 / 2 cup each)
169 calories per serving; 3 gm. protein; 39 gm. carbohydrates;
0 fat; 0 cholesterol; 4 gm. fiber; 2 mg. iron;
27 mg. calcium; 14 mg. sodium

Exchanges:
2 breads

*To balance your meal add: *Hawaiian Chicken Breasts,*
**Strawberry Salad*

*Recipe included in this book

Pack a Pocket

*P*ita bread, or what some people call pocket bread, can be used to create many fun meals. Enriched flour or whole wheat varieties are available at most supermarkets. Foods can be stuffed inside or spread on top of your pita, whatever you desire. Hot or cold foods, along with salads and casserole dishes, can be stuffed inside a pita to create a finger food. Or use your pita as a crust for a fruit or vegetable pizza. Add tomato or spaghetti sauce with vegetable toppings or low-fat cream cheese with fruit for fruit pizzas. Sliced vegetables and fruits can even be used to make faces on top of sauces and cheese. Don't forget to let your whole family pitch in and help create too. The more they do for themselves, the happier they will be, and more likely they will be to eat their own creations.

Options for stuffing:
tuna

chicken salad

egg salad

tossed salad with dressing

roast beef

sliced turkey

cheese cubes or slices

meatballs

Pita Pizzas

Fresh vegetables and fruits to try on your pita.

Vegetables	Fruits
diced onions	diced apples
sliced mushrooms	sliced bananas
fresh diced tomatoes	sliced kiwi
cherry tomatoes	orange sections
broccoli	sliced pears
chopped spinach	red, green or purple grapes
sliced zucchini	

sliced green, red or yellow peppers

- **For Vegetable Pizza:** Spread uncut pita bread with pizza or spaghetti sauce. Top with cut up vegetables and shredded mozzarella cheese. Bake at 400° for 8-10 minutes until heated through and cheese is melted.

- **For Fruited Pizza:** Spread uncut pita bread with cream cheese. Top with cut up fruit. Serve immediately or refrigerate until ready to serve.

Chicken Parmesan Pita

Try your chicken in a pita tonight. It's fast and easy to eat.
Great for a meal in a hurry.

3 chicken breasts, boneless, skinless
1 1/2 tbsp. vegetable oil
1/2 cup spaghetti sauce
2 pita breads, cut in half
1/2 cup shredded mozzarella cheese
2 tbsp. Parmesan cheese

Cut chicken in bite-sized pieces. In large skillet, heat oil and
sauté chicken until cooked through and lightly browned. Stir in
sauce. Cook until heated thoroughly. Turn off heat. Stir in mozzarella cheese.

Fill each pita half with chicken mixture. Sprinkle each with
Parmesan cheese. Serve immediately.

Servings: 4 (1/2 stuffed pita)
300 calories per serving; 28 gm. protein; 20 gm. carbohydrates;
11 gm. fat; 65 mg. cholesterol; 1 gm. fiber; 2 mg. iron;
192 mg. calcium; 414 mg. sodium

Exchanges:
1 bread, 2 1/2 meat, 1/2 vegetable, 1 1/2 fat

*To balance your meal add: *Pea Pods and Water Chestnuts,*
**Banana Berry Smoothie Oozie*

*Recipe included in this book

Tossed Salad Pita

*Have you ever thought of serving a tossed salad in a pocket?
It's a fun way to get children to learn to love salads.*

2 pita breads, cut in half
1 cup chopped lettuce, iceberg, romaine,
    spinach, or a combination
1/4 cup peppers, red, green, or yellow, chopped
1/4 cup cucumber, chopped
1/4 cup carrots, shredded
1/4 cup chickpeas
1/4 cup cheese, cheddar or mozzarella, shredded
1/2 cup low-fat salad dressing, of your choice

Cut pita bread in half. Set aside.
    Combine all salad ingredients in small bowl. Toss thoroughly.
Fill each pita pocket with salad. Sprinkle with salad dressing.

Servings: 4 (1/2 stuffed pita)
166 calories per serving; 7 gm. protein; 22 gm. carbohydrates;
5 gm. fat; 8 mg. cholesterol; 2 gm. fiber; 1 mg. iron;
114 mg. calcium; 622 mg. sodium

Exchanges:
1 bread, 1/2 meat, 1/2 fat

*To balance your meal add: *Turkey Burgers,
Strawberry Salad

Recipe included in this book

Tuna Melt in a Pocket

An old favorite made a different way.

1 pita bread
1/2 cup chunk light or white tuna
2 tbsp. light mayonnaise
1/4 cup cheese, mozzarella or cheddar, shredded

Slice pita in half circles. Combine tuna and mayonnaise. Spoon half of tuna mixture into each pocket. Sprinkle with cheese. Microwave 30 seconds to melt cheese, if desired.

Servings: 2 (1/2 stuffed pita)
195 calories per serving; 21 gm. protein; 20 gm. carbohydrates;
3 gm. fat; 25 mg. cholesterol; 0 fiber; 2 mg. iron;
123 mg. calcium; 587 mg. sodium

Exchanges:
1 bread, 1 1/2 meat

*To balance your meal add: Fresh Baby Carrots and
Sliced Celery, Low-fat Milk*

Teriyaki Meatball Pita

You can also make this recipe in a loaf pan.

1 lb. lean ground beef
1/2 cup plain bread crumbs
1/2 cup honey-teriyaki flavored barbecue sauce, divided
1 egg
1/2 tsp. pepper
4 large pita breads

Preheat oven to 400°. Combine beef, bread crumbs, 1/4 cup barbecue sauce, egg, and pepper in mixing bowl. Using about 2 tablespoons of beef at a time, roll meat into balls. Place balls in 9" x 11" baking dish. Pour remaining barbecue sauce over top. Bake 20 minutes or until beef is cooked through and no longer pink. Cut each pita in half. Spoon meatballs into pocket just before serving.

Servings: 8
253 calories per serving; 17 gm. protein; 23 gm. carbohydrates;
9 gm. fat; 69 mg. cholesterol; 1 gm. fiber; 3 mg. iron;
58 mg. calcium; 380 mg. sodium

Exchanges:
1 1/2 bread, 2 meat, 1 fat

To balance your meal add: Tossed Salad with Low-fat Dressing,
*Rainbow Fruit Sticks

*Recipe included in this book

Peanut Butter Pita Surprise

Here's a fun way to jazz up your peanut butter sandwich.

1/4 cup peanut butter
1/4 cup mashed banana or apple
1 large pita bread, cut in half

Combine peanut butter with chopped fruit. Spoon into pita pocket. Serve immediately.

Servings: 2
296 calories per serving; 11 gm. protein; 30 gm. carbohydrates;
16 gm. fat; 0 cholesterol; 3 gm. fiber; 1 mg. iron;
38 mg. calcium; 313 mg. sodium

Exchanges:
1 bread, 1 meat, 1 fruit, 2 fat

To balance your meal add: *Banana Berry Smoothie Oozie

*Recipe included in this book

Create a Stir

Stir-frying has become a very popular way to cook. It is quick, easy, and requires little or no fat. You can create your own meal in minutes with little effort by combining various combinations of meats and vegetables. Add hot cooked rice or pasta to finish off your meal.

Prepare your Skillet or Wok

- Start with a large nonstick skillet or wok and coat with vegetable oil cooking spray or a small amount of vegetable oil, broth, wine, vinegar or water.

- Cut your foods before heating your skillet or wok, so you are ready to cook. Small, uniform-sized pieces of foods are easiest to cook.

- Heat skillet or wok over medium-high heat. Have the appropriate spatulas ready and be prepared to stir foods frequently.

- Some meats may require more cooking than vegetables in order to cook thoroughly. If this is the case, begin cooking meats first, before adding the vegetables.

Options for Stir-Fry:

Meat

beef
chicken
shrimp
turkey

Sauces

sweet and sour sauce
teriyaki sauce
soy sauce
Worchestershire sauce
wine

Vegetables

broccoli
cauliflower
peppers
celery
carrots
pea pods
onions
mushrooms

Shrimp and Pepper Stir-Fry

Try this stir-fry over hot linguini.

2 tbsp. vegetable oil
1 pound uncooked shrimp, shelled and deveined
1 1/2 tsp. lemon pepper seasoning
1 tsp. garlic powder
1 tsp. crushed dry basil
4 tsp. vinegar
1/2 cup green pepper, chopped
1/2 cup red pepper, chopped
1/2 cup yellow pepper, chopped

Heat oil in large skillet or wok over medium-high heat. Add shrimp, spices, and vinegar and sauté 3-5 minutes. Add vegetables. Sauté an additional 2 minutes until peppers are tender.

Servings: 4 (1/2 cup each)
197 calories per serving; 24 gm. protein; 5 gm. carbohydrates;
9 gm. fat; 173 mg. cholesterol; 1 gm. fiber; 3 mg. iron;
73 mg. calcium; 169 mg. sodium

Exchanges:
3 1/2 meat, 1/2 vegetable, 1 1/2 fat

To balance your meal add: Hot Linguini, *Apple Pudding

*Recipe included in this book

Chick'n Pepper Stir-Fry

You can't get much easier than this. And it's color will attract any appetite, small or large. Try it with hot cooked rice.

1 tbsp. vegetable oil
3 chicken breasts, boneless, skinless, sliced in strips
1 red pepper, thinly sliced
1 green pepper, thinly sliced
1 yellow pepper, thinly sliced
2 cloves garlic, minced
1 tbsp. soy sauce

Heat oil in large skillet or wok over medium-high heat. Add chicken and sauté 2-3 minutes until cooked through. Add peppers and garlic. Sauté an additional 5 minutes until peppers are tender. Remove from heat. Stir in soy sauce.

Servings: 4 (1/2 cup each)

154 calories per serving; 22 gm. protein; 6 gm. carbohydrates;
5 gm. fat; 51 mg. cholesterol; 1 gm. fiber; 1 mg. iron;
22 mg. calcium; 316 mg. sodium

Exchanges:
2 meat, 1 vegetable, 1/2 fat

To balance your meal add: Steamed Rice, *Fruit Ambrosia

*Recipe included in this book

Garlic Chicken Stir-Fry

A quick and tasty meal for stir-fry (and garlic) lovers.

3 chicken breasts, boneless, skinless, chopped
    or sliced in strips
2 tbsp. cornstarch
1 tbsp. cooking wine (or water)
2 cloves garlic, minced
1 cup chicken broth
4 tsp. vinegar
1/2 tsp. crushed red pepper
2 tbsp. vegetable oil
2 carrots, thinly sliced
1 cup broccoli, chopped
3 tbsp. soy sauce

Coat chicken with 1 tbsp. of the cornstarch, wine (or water), and garlic. Set aside.

Combine broth, vinegar, red pepper, and remaining 1 tbsp. of the cornstarch. Set aside.

Heat 1 tbsp. of the oil in large skillet or wok over medium-high heat. Add chicken and sauté 2-3 minutes until cooked through. Remove from skillet.

Heat remaining 1 tbsp. of the oil. Add vegetables and sauté 2-3 minutes until tender-crisp. Add chicken back to vegetables. Pour broth mixture over. Cook until sauce thickens and boils. Remove from heat. Stir in soy sauce.

Servings: 4 (1 / 2 cup each)
217 calories per serving; 24 gm. protein; 11 gm. carbohydrates;
8 gm. fat; 51 gm. cholesterol; 2 gm. fiber; 1 mg. iron;
38 mg. calcium; 1041 mg. sodium

Exchanges:
2 meat, 1 vegetable, 1 1/2 fat

*To balance your meal add: Hot Pasta,
French Bread, *Strawberry Sorbet*

Recipe included in this book

Beef and Broccoli Stir-Fry

1 pound beef flank steak
1/4 cup water
2 tbsp. soy sauce
2 tbsp. dry sherry
1 1/2 tsp. cornstarch
1 garlic clove, minced
1/2 tsp. crushed red pepper
1 tbsp. vegetable oil
1 cup broccoli, chopped

Slice slightly frozen flank steak into bite-sized pieces. Set aside.
Combine water, soy sauce, sherry, cornstarch, garlic, and red
pepper. Set aside.

Heat oil in large skillet or wok. Add beef. Stir-fry 3-4 minutes
or until cooked through. Add broccoli. Stir-fry until broccoli is
tender-crisp. Stir sauce and add to mixture. Stir until thickened.
Cook on medium heat for 1-2 minutes. Serve over rice, if desired.

Servings: 4 (1/2 cup each)
233 calories per serving; 25 gm. protein; 5 gm. carbohydrates;
12 gm. fat; 57 mg. cholesterol; 1 gm. fiber; 3 mg. iron;
31 mg. calcium; 597 mg. sodium

Exchanges:
3 meat, 1/2 vegetable, 1 fat

To balance your meal add: Steamed Brown Rice,
*Quick and Easy Carrot Cake
*Recipe included in this book

Chicken and Broccoli Oriental
(Microwave)

Here's a new twist to stir-frying. Try it in your microwave.
It's just as fast, and clean up is a breeze.

3 chicken breasts, boneless, skinless
1 tbsp. teriyaki sauce
1 tbsp. vinegar
1 tbsp. molasses
1 clove garlic, minced
1/4 tsp. crushed red pepper, optional
1 cup carrots, sliced
4 cups fresh broccoli, chopped
1 1/2 tsp. cornstarch
1 tbsp. water

Slice chicken breasts into bite-sized pieces. In 2-quart microwave-safe casserole dish, combine teriyaki sauce, vinegar, molasses, garlic, and red pepper. Add chicken. Let marinate for 10 minutes.

Microwave meat mixture, covered, on high for 2-3 minutes until chicken is tender and cooked throughout. Stir half way through. Remove chicken from casserole and set aside. Retain marinade in casserole dish.

Add carrots to casserole dish. Cook, covered, on high for 1 minute. Add broccoli. Cover and cook an additional 3-4 minutes, until vegetables are tender-crisp.

Stir cornstarch into water. Add to vegetables. Cook, uncovered, on high for 1-2 minutes until juices are slightly thickened, stirring half way through.

Add chicken to vegetables. Cook, covered, on high for 1 minute to heat through.

Servings: 4 (1 cup each)
160 calories per serving; 23 gm. protein; 12 gm. carbohydrates;
3 gm. fat; 55 mg. cholesterol; 3 gm. fiber; 2 mg. iron;
70 mg. calcium; 337 mg. sodium

Exchanges:
2 meat, 1 vegetable

*To balance your meal add: Hot Angel Hair Pasta,
Peanut Butter Cup Cookies

Quick Pepper Steak

A hearty meal made in just minutes.

1 pound boneless sirloin steak
2 tbsp. vegetable oil
10 3/4-oz. can condensed beef broth
1 medium onion, sliced

Recipe included in this book

2 medium green peppers, sliced
1/2 tsp. garlic powder
1/2 tsp. salt
1/2 tsp. ginger
1 tbsp. cornstarch
2 tsp. sugar
2 tbsp. soy sauce
2 medium tomatoes, peeled and cut into wedges

While partially frozen, slice steak into 2-inch strips. Heat oil in large skillet over medium heat. Cook steak, approximately 4-6 minutes until browned. Add broth, onion, peppers, garlic powder, salt, and ginger. Simmer for 5 minutes.

Combine cornstarch, sugar, and soy sauce, stirring well. Add to beef mixture. Bring to boil. Continue boiling for 1 minute, stirring constantly. Remove from heat. Add tomatoes. Toss gently. Serve with or over rice.

Servings: 8 (3/4 cup each)
149 calories per serving; 15 gm. protein; 7 gm. carbohydrates;
7 gm. fat; 38 mg. cholesterol; 1 gm. fiber; 2 mg. iron;
17 mg. calcium; 701 mg. sodium

Exchanges:
1 1/2 meat, 1/2 vegetable, 1/2 fat

To balance your meal add: Steamed Rice,
*Chinese Coleslaw

*Recipe included in this book

Salads and Such

Confetti Chicken Salad

1/4 cup low-fat cottage cheese
8-oz. can crushed pineapple, drained
2 tbsp. mayonnaise
1 tsp. sugar
1/8 tsp. ginger
2 tsp. lemon juice
3 cups cooked chicken, chopped
3/4 cup seedless grapes, red or green or a combination
3/4 cup water chestnuts, sliced
1 tbsp. chives, chopped
1/2 cup mandarin oranges

Blend cottage cheese, pineapple, mayonnaise, sugar, ginger, and lemon juice in a food processor or blender until smooth. Combine chicken, grapes, water chestnuts, and chives in large bowl. Fold cottage cheese mixture into chicken mixture. Add oranges. Chill until ready to serve. Serve on a bed of lettuce or in a pita.

Servings: 4 (1 cup each)
253 calories per serving; 23 gm. protein; 22 gm. carbohydrates;
8 gm. fat; 60 mg. cholesterol; 2 gm. fiber; 1 mg. iron;
37 mg. calcium; 150 mg. sodium

Exchanges:
2 meat, 1 fruit, 1/2 vegetable, 1 fat

*To balance your meal add: *Cranberry Muffins, Low-fat Milk*

Recipe included in this book

Molded Apple and Cheese Salad

A cool salad that's great with summer meals. Make it the night before or in the morning. It only takes several minutes to prepare.

3-oz. package cherry gelatin
1 1/2 cups boiling water
3-oz. package low-fat cream cheese
8-oz. can juice-packed crushed pineapple
1 1/4 cups apple, finely chopped
1/2 cup chopped nuts, optional

Dissolve gelatin into boiling water. Cool.

Mix cream cheese with 1/3 cup drained pineapple juice. Add pineapple, apple, and nuts, if desired. Combine with gelatin mixture and mix thoroughly. Pour into 9"x 12" casserole dish or gelatin mold. Chill until firm.

Servings: 8 (3/4 cup each)
91 calories per serving; 2 gm. protein; 17 gm. carbohydrates;
2 gm. fat; 6 mg. cholesterol; 0 fiber; 0 iron;
17 mg. calcium; 59 mg. sodium

Exchanges:
1 fruit, 1/2 fat

To balance your meal add: *Dutch Oven Chicken, Low-fat Milk

*Recipe included in this book

Strawberry Salad

*Gelatin salads are a real treat for kids. Plan ahead
and whip this one up in a flash for tonight's meal.*

3-oz. package raspberry gelatin
1 cup boiling water
8-oz. can juice packed crushed pineapple
1 pint frozen strawberries
1 cup low-fat sour cream

Dissolve gelatin in boiling water. Add fruit. Pour half of the gelatin
mixture into a 8" x 8" pan. Chill until firm. Keep remaining gelatin
at room temperature.

Spread sour cream over firm gelatin. Pour remaining gelatin
over sour cream. Chill again until firm. Cut into squares before
serving.

Servings: 8 (2"x 4" rectangle)
106 calories per serving; 2 gm. protein; 17 gm. carbohydrates;
4 gm. fat; 12 mg. cholesterol; 1 gm. fiber; 0 iron;
41 mg. calcium; 40 mg. sodium

Exchanges:
1 fruit, 1/2 fat

*To balance your meal add: *Turkey Burgers,
Steamed String Beans*

*Recipe included in this book

Ice Cream Fruit Salad

A treat for kids of all ages—moms and dads, too.

3-oz. package strawberry gelatin
(or any desired flavor)
1 cup boiling water
1 pint vanilla ice milk
16-oz. can juice packed fruit cocktail, drained

Dissolve gelatin in boiling water. Add ice milk and stir until dissolved. Add drained fruit cocktail.

Pour mixture into gelatin mold or 9" x 12" pan. Chill until firm.

Servings: 8 (3" x 4 1/2" rectangle)
112 calories per serving; 2 gm. protein; 24 gm. carbohydrates;
1 gm. fat; 5 mg. cholesterol; 1 gm. fiber; 0 iron;
51 mg. calcium; 57 mg. sodium

Exchanges:
1 fruit

To balance your meal add: *Macaroni and Chili,
*Gingersnaps

*Recipe included in this book

Chinese Coleslaw

A new twist to an old favorite. Bok choy (Chinese cabbage),
water chestnuts, and pineapple make this dish unique.

8-oz. can sliced water chestnuts
4 cups bok choy, shredded
1/2 cup fresh parsley, chopped
8-oz. can crushed pineapple, drained
1/4 cup onion, chopped
1/4 cup low-fat mayonnaise
1/2 tsp. ginger

Combine water chestnuts, bok choy, parsley, pineapple, and onion in large bowl. Stir together mayonnaise and ginger. Toss into coleslaw.

Servings: 8 (3/4 cup)
45 calories per serving; 1 gm. protein; 11 gm. carbohydrates;
0 fat; 0 cholesterol; 1 gm. fiber; 1 mg. iron;
48 mg. calcium; 112 mg. sodium

Exchanges:
1/2 fruit, 1 vegetable

*To balance your meal add: *Tangy Marinated Flank Steak,*
Brown Rice

*Recipe included in this book

Apple Fruit Salad

Make the yogurt dressing in a squirt bottle and let your little ones drizzle their own on. This is a fun treat anytime.

1 golden delicious apple, cored, peeled and sliced
1 red delicious apple, cored, peeled and sliced
1 small banana, peeled and sliced
16 seedless red grapes
1/4 cup plain nonfat yogurt
1 tbsp. orange juice
1/4 tsp. cinnamon

Mix all cut up fruits together. Spoon into small bowls or custard cups. Combine yogurt, orange juice, and cinnamon in small bowl. Drizzle over fruit before serving.

Servings: 4 (1/2 cup)
89 calories per serving; 1 gm. protein; 22 gm. carbohydrates;
0 fat; 0 cholesterol; 2 gm. fiber; 0 iron;
39 mg. calcium; 12 mg. sodium

Exchanges:
1 fruit

*To balance your meal add: *Lazy Day Beef Pie,
Fresh Baby Carrot Sticks*

*Recipe included in this book

Pasta Salad

*Variations of this salad are endless. Try it with any
number of vegetables, or even add tuna or chicken.
You can even make it lower in fat with a nonfat dressing.*

1 pound spiral pasta
6-oz. jar marinated artichokes
1 cup green pepper, chopped
1 cup red pepper, chopped
1/2 cup green onion, chopped
8-oz. bottle low-calorie Italian dressing
2 tbsp. Parmesan cheese

Cook pasta according to package directions. Drain and place into
large bowl. Add artichokes, vegetables, and salad dressing.
Refrigerate overnight. Sprinkle with Parmesan cheese just before
serving.

Servings: 8 (3/4 cup each)
147 calories per serving; 4 gm. protein; 21 gm. carbohydrates;
5 gm. fat; 1 mg. cholesterol; 2 gm. fiber; 1 mg. iron;
38 mg. calcium; 367 mg. sodium

Exchanges:
1 bread, 1/2 vegetable, 1 1/2 fat

*To balance your meal add: *Quick Vegetable Pizza,
Low-fat Milk*

Recipe included in this book

Fruit Ambrosia

Jazz up any dinner party with a colorful fruit dish such as this.

2 cups orange sections
1 cup pink grapefruit sections
8-oz. can juice packed pineapple chunks
1/2 cup flaked coconut
2 tbsp. honey

Arrange half of the orange sections in a glass bowl. Top with grapefruit sections, pineapple, 1/4 cup of the coconut, and remaining orange sections. Drizzle with honey. Sprinkle with remaining coconut. Cover and chill until ready to serve.

Servings: 6 (3/4 cup each)
130 calories per serving; 1 gm. protein; 24 gm. carbohydrates;
4 gm. fat; 0 cholesterol; 2 gm. fiber; 1 mg. iron;
21 mg. calcium; 7 mg. sodium

Exchanges:
1 1/2 fruit, 1/2 fat

*To balance your meal add: *Tuna and Egg a la King,
Fresh Pepper Slices*

Recipe included in this book

Turkey Apple Salad

1 1/2 cups cooked turkey, cut into strips
2 apples, unpeeled and diced
2 tbsp. vegetable oil
2 tbsp. white wine vinegar
1/2 tsp. dry mustard
1/4 tsp. ginger
1/8 tsp. pepper
3 cups torn lettuce leaves
2 tbsp. toasted slivered almonds

Combine turkey and apple in large bowl. Set aside. Combine oil, vinegar, mustard, ginger, and pepper in small bowl. Pour dressing over turkey and apples, tossing to coat well. Cover and refrigerate until chilled. Just before serving, add lettuce and almonds to turkey. Toss well.

Servings: 4 (1 cup each)
208 calories per serving; 17 gm. protein; 13 gm. carbohydrates;
10 gm. fat; 45 mg. cholesterol; 2 gm. fiber; 2 mg. iron;
53 mg. calcium; 34 mg. sodium

Exchanges:
1 1/2 meat, 1 fruit, 1 1/2 fat

*To balance your meal add: *Parmesan Garlic Bread,
Low-fat Chocolate Milk*

Recipe included in this book

Jiffy Fruit Salad

This fruit salad makes a wonderful accompaniment to any meal, and you can make it in a "jiffy."

16-oz. can fruit cocktail
20-oz. can pineapple chunks
1 small package strawberry gelatin
8-oz. carton low-fat sour cream
8-oz. carton frozen whipped topping, thawed

Drain fruit cocktail and pineapple chunks. Place fruit in bowl. Sprinkle fruit with dry gelatin. Stir in sour cream and whipped topping. Mix well. Pour into mold. Refrigerate until ready to serve.

Servings: 12 (1/2 cup)
158 calories per serving; 2 gm. protein; 23 gm. carbohydrates;
7 gm. fat; 7 mg. cholesterol; 1 gm. fiber; 0 iron;
31 mg. calcium; 32 mg. sodium

Exchanges:
1 fruit, 1 1/2 fat

*To balance your meal add: *Quick Pepper Steak, Rice Pilaf*

*Recipe included in this book

In the Bread Basket

Blueberry Muffins

1 1/2 cups flour
1/4 cup sugar
1 tbsp. baking powder
1 1/2 cups corn flake cereal
1 cup low-fat milk
1 egg
1/4 cup vegetable oil
1 cup blueberries, fresh or frozen
Vegetable oil cooking spray

Preheat oven to 400°. In small bowl, mix flour, sugar, and baking powder. In large bowl, add milk to cereal. Let soften 2-3 minutes.

Beat egg. Add egg and oil to cereal mixture. Stir in flour mixture. Add blueberries.

Spray muffin tins with vegetable oil cooking spray. Pour batter into tins. Bake for 15-20 minutes or until golden brown.

Servings: 12 muffins
148 calories per muffin; 3 gm. protein; 21 gm. carbohydrates;
6 gm. fat; 19 mg. cholesterol; 1 gm. fiber; 1 mg. iron;
30 mg. calcium; 48 mg. sodium

Exchanges:
1 bread, 1/2 fruit, 1 fat

*To balance your meal add: *Tomato Mushroom Frittata,
Low-fat Milk*

Recipe included in this book

Raisin Bran Muffins

2 cups Raisin Bran® cereal
1/2 cup sugar
1 1/4 cups flour
1/2 tsp. salt
1 1/4 tsp. baking soda
1 egg
1/4 cup vegetable oil
1 cup buttermilk

Preheat oven to 375°.

Combine cereal, sugar, flour, salt and soda in large mixing bowl. Beat the egg slightly. Add egg, oil, and buttermilk to dry mixture. Mix only until dry ingredients are moistened.

Spoon batter evenly into muffin tins, filling each approximately half full. Bake 20-25 minutes. Serve warm.

Servings: 12 large or 36 mini-muffins
163 calories per large muffin; 4 gm. protein; 26 gm. carbohydrates;
5 gm. fat; 18 mg. cholesterol; 1 gm. fiber; 5 mg. iron;
31 mg. calcium; 253 mg. sodium

Exchanges:
1 bread, 1/2 fruit, 1 fat

*To balance your meal add: *Indian Corn Stew,
Chilled Fruit Cocktail*

Recipe included in this book

Oatmeal Muffins

1 cup rolled oats
1 cup buttermilk
1/3 cup margarine
1/2 cup brown sugar
1 egg
1 cup flour
1 tsp. baking powder
1/2 tsp. baking soda
1 tsp. salt
Vegetable oil cooking spray

Soak oats in buttermilk for 1 hour. Preheat oven to 400°.

Blend margarine, brown sugar, and egg. Sift together flour, baking powder, soda, and salt. Combine flour mixture alternately with oats mixture into margarine-sugar mixture.

Spray muffin tins with vegetable oil cooking spray. Fill tins with mixture 2/3 full. Bake 20-25 minutes. Serve hot.

Servings: 12 muffins
146 calories per muffin; 3 gm. protein; 19 gm. carbohydrates;
6 gm. fat; 18 mg. cholesterol; 1 gm. fiber; 1 mg. iron;
38 mg. calcium; 300 mg. sodium

Exchanges:
1 bread

*To balance your meal add: *Zucchini Pizza, Fresh Fruit Cup*

Recipe included in this book

Cranberry Muffins

To reduce the fat and cholesterol even more,
try 1/2 cup egg substitute in place of the 2 eggs.

1 cup chopped cranberries
1/2 cup sugar, divided
1 3/4 cups flour
2 tsp. baking powder
3/4 cup low-fat milk
2 eggs
1 tsp. grated orange peel, optional
1/4 cup melted margarine
1/2 tsp. cinnamon

Preheat oven to 400°. In small bowl, combine cranberries and 2 tbsp. of sugar. Let stand for 5 minutes. In large bowl, combine flour, baking powder, and 4 tbsp. of sugar. In another small bowl, blend milk, eggs, and orange peel, if desired.

Alternately, add milk mixture and margarine to flour mixture until just moistened. Stir in cranberries.

Spoon batter evenly into muffin tins, filling each about half full. Combine remaining sugar with cinnamon. Sprinkle over tops of muffins. Bake 12-15 minutes or until brown. Serve warm.

Servings: 12 large or 36 mini-muffins
157 calories per large muffin; 3 gm. protein; 24 gm. carbohydrates;
5 gm. fat; 36 mg. cholesterol; 1 gm. fiber; 1 mg. iron;
29 mg. calcium; 63 mg. sodium

Exchanges:
1 bread, 1/2 fruit

To balance your meal add: *Chicken and Vegetable Pasta

Chunky Apple Muffins

*This will be a favorite in your household. Great for lunch boxes
and after school snacks. You can even double the recipe and
freeze the extra for later.*

3/4 cup sugar
1/4 cups oil
1/2 cup low-fat milk
2 eggs
1 tsp. vanilla extract
2 apples, peeled, cored and diced
1 1/2 cups flour
2 tsp. baking powder

*Recipe included in this book

1/2 tsp. baking soda
1/2 tsp. cinnamon
1/4 tsp. salt
Vegetable oil cooking spray

Preheat oven to 375°. In large bowl, combine sugar, oil, milk, eggs, and vanilla. Beat until smooth. Add remaining ingredients. Mix until just combined. Spoon batter about 2/3 full into muffin tins sprayed with vegetable oil cooking spray. Bake 20-25 minutes until browned.

Servings: 15 large or 30 mini-muffins
140 calories per large muffin; 2 gm. protein; 22 gm. carbohydrates;
5 gm. fat; 29 mg. cholesterol; 1 gm. fiber; 1 mg. iron;
16 mg. calcium; 76 mg. sodium

Exchanges:
1/2 bread, 1 fruit, 1 fat

To balance your meal add: Peanut Butter and Applesauce
Sandwich, Low-fat Chocolate Milk

Yummy Bran Muffins

3 cups All Bran® cereal
1 cup boiling water
2 1/2 cups flour
2 1/2 tsp. baking soda
1 1/2 cups brown sugar
1/2 cup vegetable oil
2 eggs, slightly beaten
2 cups buttermilk

Preheat oven to 400°. Add All Bran to boiling water. Let sit for at least 3 minutes. Combine flour, soda, and brown sugar in mixing bowl. Set aside. Combine oil, eggs, and buttermilk in large mixing bowl. Add cereal mixture to oil, eggs, and milk. Add dry ingredients and mix well. Do not beat.

Spoon mixture into muffin tins and bake for 15-18 minutes. (If you use mini-muffin tins, they will take less time to bake.)

Servings: 36 muffins
120 calories per muffin; 3 gm. protein; 21 gm. carbohydrates;
4 gm. fat; 11 mg. cholesterol; 3 gm. fiber; 2 mg. iron;
30 mg. calcium; 174 mg. sodium

Exchanges:
1/2 bread, 1/2 fruit, 1/2 fat

*To balance your meal add: *Dutch Oven Chicken,
Steamed Broccoli Spears*

Recipe included in this book

Cinnamon Applesauce Muffins

These are great for breakfast or after school.

1 cup flour
1/3 cup firmly packed brown sugar
1 tsp. cinnamon
3/4 cup wheat germ
1 tbsp. baking powder
1/2 cup low-fat milk
3 tbsp. vegetable oil
1 cup applesauce
2 egg whites, slightly beaten
Vegetable oil cooking spray

Preheat oven to 400°. Lightly spray bottoms of muffin tins with vegetable oil cooking spray. Combine flour, brown sugar, cinnamon, wheat germ, and baking powder. Add remaining ingredients. Mix just until dry ingredients are moistened. Fill muffin cups 2/3 full. Bake 15-20 minutes or until golden brown.

Servings: 12 large or 24 mini-muffins
114 calories per large muffin; 3 gm. protein; 17 gm. carbohydrates;
4 gm. fat; 0 cholesterol; 1 gm. fiber; 1 mg. iron;
22 mg. calcium; 17 mg. sodium

Exchanges:
1/2 bread, 1/2 fruit, 1 fat

To balance your meal add: *Dump Soup

*Recipe included in this book

Cinnamon French Toast

This works great with any type of bread (even day old bread) and tastes great with low-calorie syrup, jams, or fruit spreads.

2 eggs
1/4 cup low-fat milk
1/2 tsp. vanilla extract
1/2 tsp. cinnamon
1/4 tsp. nutmeg
Vegetable oil cooking spray
8 slices Italian bread

In small bowl, mix together eggs, milk, vanilla, cinnamon, and nutmeg. Set aside. Over medium heat, preheat nonstick skillet, sprayed with vegetable oil cooking spray. Dip bread in egg mixture and place in prepared skillet. Cook until golden brown, about 1-2 minutes on each side. Serve warm.

Servings: 8 (1 slice per serving)
120 calories per serving; 5 gm. protein; 19 gm. carbohydrates;
2 gm. fat; 54 mg. cholesterol; 1 gm. fiber; 1 mg. iron;
43 mg. calcium; 233 mg. sodium

Exchanges:
1 bread

*To balance your meal add: Canadian Bacon, Fresh Melon Balls,
Low-fat Milk*

Parmesan Garlic Bread

Try these with a bowl of hot soup on a cold night.

1 loaf French bread
2 tbsp. olive oil
4 cloves garlic, minced
2 tbsp. Parmesan cheese
1/2 tsp. oregano or Italian seasoning
1/4 tsp. ground black pepper

Preheat oven to 400°. Slice bread into 1/2" slices. Lay slices flat on cookie sheet. Brush top side with oil. Sprinkle on garlic, Parmesan cheese, oregano, and pepper. Bake approximately 5 minutes until lightly browned.

Servings: 16 slices
97 calories per slice; 3 gm. protein; 15 gm. carbohydrates;
3 gm. fat; 1 mg. cholesterol; 1 gm. fiber; 1 mg. iron;
34 mg. calcium; 187 mg. sodium

Exchanges:
1 bread, 1/2 fat

*To balance your meal add: *Italian Vegetable Soup,
Chilled Pineapple Slices*

*Recipe included in this book

Broccoli Cornbread

Kids love cornbread. Why not make it more nutritious and add some broccoli? They will love it.

10-oz. package frozen, chopped broccoli
1 box Jiffy® cornbread mix
4 eggs
1/4 cup onion, chopped
1/2 cup cheddar cheese, shredded
Vegetable oil cooking spray

Preheat oven to 350°. Cook broccoli in microwave oven according to package directions. Drain. Combine broccoli with remaining ingredients. Pour into 13" x 9" baking dish sprayed with vegetable oil cooking spray.

Bake 25-30 minutes or until top is golden brown.

Servings: 16 (2 1/2" x 4 1/2" slice)
80 calories per serving; 4 gm. protein; 7 gm. carbohydrates;
4 gm. fat; 62 mg. cholesterol; 1 gm. fiber; 1 mg. iron;
61 mg. calcium; 157 mg. sodium

Exchanges:
1/2 bread, 1/2 meat, 1/2 vegetable, 1/2 fat

*To balance your meal add: *Porcupine Meatballs,
Cinnamon Carrots, Chilled Watermelon Slice

Recipe included in this book

Gumdrop Bread

Your little ones will marvel over this fun, colorful bread.
You'll have a great time making it for them.

3/4 cup tiny gumdrops
3 cups flour
3/4 cup sugar
1 tbsp. baking powder
1/4 tsp. salt
1/2 cup walnut pieces, optional
1 egg
1/3 cup vegetable oil
1 1/3 cups low-fat milk
1/2 tsp. vanilla extract
Vegetable oil cooking spray

Preheat oven to 350°. Place gumdrops, flour, sugar, baking powder, salt, and walnut pieces, if desired, in large mixing bowl. Beat egg just until the white and yolk are mixed. Add egg, oil, milk, and vanilla to dry mixture. Stir until dry ingredients are just wet. The mixture will be lumpy. DO NOT OVERMIX.

Spray loaf pan with vegetable oil cooking spray. Pour batter into pan. Bake 60-65 minutes or until golden brown.

Servings: 12 slices
243 calories per slice; 5 gm. protein; 41 gm. carbohydrates;
7 gm. fat; 18 mg. cholesterol; 1 gm. fiber; 1 mg. iron;
40 mg. calcium; 66 mg. sodium

Exchanges:
1 bread, 1 fruit, 1 fat

To balance your meal add: Macaroni and Cheese,
Baby Carrot Sticks

Apple Juice (Cider) Biscuits

Here's a new breakfast idea that everyone is sure to rave about.

2 cups biscuit mix
2 tbsp. sugar
1/2 tsp. cinnamon
1/2 cup walnut pieces, optional
1 small apple
1/2 cup apple juice or cider
Vegetable oil cooking spray

Preheat oven to 450°. Measure biscuit mix, sugar, and cinnamon into large mixing bowl. Place walnut pieces, if desired, in a plastic bag or between two pieces of waxed paper. With a rolling pin, crush the walnut pieces into "meal-like" consistency. Stir into dry ingredients.

Wash apple and shred it (or grate it) finely, throwing away the core and seeds. Add apple to dry mixture. Pour juice into dry mixture stirring only until mixture is wet. Batter will be lumpy. DO NOT OVERMIX.

Drop the biscuit dough onto a cookie sheet that has been sprayed with vegetable oil cooking spray. To drop dough, use a large spoon or small ice cream scooper and push the dough off with a smaller spoon. Bake 10-12 minutes or until golden brown. Serve hot.

Servings: 12 biscuits
115 calories per biscuit; 2 gm. protein; 19 gm. carbohydrates;
3 gm. fat; 1 mg. cholesterol; 1 gm. fiber; 1 mg. iron;
55 mg. calcium; 271 mg. sodium

Exchanges:
1 bread, 1/2 fruit, 1/2 fat

To balance your meal add: Hard-Cooked Egg, Fresh Melon Wedge,
Low-fat Milk

Apple Biscuits

1/3 cup light brown sugar
2 tbsp. flour
1/2 tsp. cinnamon
10-oz. can refrigerated biscuits
Vegetable oil cooking spray
1/2 cup shredded mild cheddar cheese
2 large apples, cored and cut into rings
1 tbsp. melted margarine

Preheat oven to 400°. Combine brown sugar, flour, and cinnamon in small bowl. Set aside. Separate each biscuit and press each into a 3" circle on a cookie sheet sprayed with vegetable oil cooking spray. Sprinkle each circle with shredded cheese and top with apple ring. Sprinkle with sugar mixture and drizzle with melted margarine. Bake 12-15 minutes or until crust is golden brown. Serve immediately.

Servings: 10 biscuits
158 calories per biscuit; 3 gm. protein; 23 gm. carbohydrates;
6 gm. fat; 7 mg. cholesterol; 2 gm. fiber; 1 mg. iron;
92 mg. calcium; 267 mg. sodium

Exchanges:
1 bread, 1 fruit, 1 fat

*To balance your meal add: *All-American Meatballs,
Lettuce and Tomato Salad*

Recipe included in this book

Flower Garden Biscuits

*Have fun creating your own biscuits for breakfast,
brunch, or just for fun. Children love being involved.*

10-oz. can refrigerated biscuits
10 tsp. favorite jelly or jam

Separate biscuits. Place on nonstick cookie sheet.

Flatten each biscuit slightly. With kitchen scissors cut four or
five slices around the edge of each biscuit (cut from outside to
center of biscuit leaving space in the center of each.) Press your
thumb in the center of each biscuit to make a hole. Spoon 1 tsp.
jelly in center of each. Bake according to package directions
(usually at 425°).

Servings: 10 biscuits
113 calories per biscuit; 2 gm. protein; 18 gm. carbohydrates;
3 gm. fat; 1 mg. cholesterol; 0 fiber; 1 mg. iron;
54 mg. calcium; 272 mg. sodium

Exchanges:
1 bread, 1/2 fat

*To balance your meal add: Scrambled Eggs,
Hash Brown Potato Casserole, Chilled Orange Juice

Recipe included in this book

Pumpkin Pancakes

*Try this pancake recipe that's rich in vitamin A and
beta-carotene. Cooked or canned carrots, sweet potatoes, or
squash may be substituted for the pumpkin.*

2 eggs
2 1/2 cups low-fat milk
1 cup canned pumpkin
3 cups biscuit mix
1 tsp. cinnamon
Vegetable oil cooking spray

In large bowl, beat eggs slightly and mix with milk. Stir in pumpkin. Add dry biscuit mix. Mix well.

Spray large skillet with vegetable oil cooking spray and heat over medium heat. (The skillet is hot enough when a drop of water sizzles on top.) Cook pancakes on both sides until golden brown.

Servings: 8 (3 small pancakes)
76 calories per serving; 2 gm. protein; 8 gm. carbohydrates;
4 gm. fat; 17 mg. cholesterol; 0 fiber; 1 mg. iron;
67 mg. calcium; 79 mg. sodium

Exchanges:
1 bread

*To balance your meal add: Fresh Fruit Cup,
Low-fat Chocolate Milk*

*Recipe included in this book

Finishing Touches

Vanilla Tea Cookies

These cookies will satisfy every sweet tooth.
And, they are low-fat too.

1 1/2 cups flour
1 cup sugar
1/2 cup margarine, softened
1 tsp. vanilla extract
1/2 tsp. baking powder
1 egg

Preheat oven to 350°. Beat together all ingredients until well blended. Take a teaspoon of dough and roll it into a ball. Place onto ungreased cookie sheet. Flatten each ball down with hand or spatula. Bake 10-12 minutes or until lightly browned around edges.

Servings: 4 dozen cookies
49 calories per cookie; 1 gm. protein; 7 gm. carbohydrates;
2 gm. fat; 4 mg. cholesterol; 0 fiber; 0 iron;
2 mg. calcium; 24 mg. sodium

Exchanges:
1/2 bread, 1/2 fruit (for 2 cookies)

*To balance your meal add: *Quick Chili Con Carne,*
Chilled Sliced Peaches

*Recipe included in this book

Peanut Butter Cup Cookies

Try these for birthday parties or other special festivities.
Your kids will want to help make them.

20-oz. roll plain sugar cookie dough
(use refrigerated commercial dough or
cookie dough you make at home)
36 mini-sized peanut butter cups

Preheat oven to 325°. Cut cookie dough into 1/4" slices. Cut each slice into quarters. Place each quarter in mini-muffin tin. Bake 8 minutes, or until cookies are beginning to brown. Remove from oven. Immediately, press 1 mini-size peanut butter cup into middle of each cookie. Cool and remove from muffin tins.

Servings: 3 dozen cookies
97 calories per cookie; 1 gm. protein; 12 gm. carbohydrates;
5 gm. fat; 5 mg. cholesterol; 0 fiber; 0 iron;
17 mg. calcium; 80 mg. sodium

Exchanges:
1/2 bread, 1 fat

To balance your meal add: *Tomato Green Chili Tortilla Casserole,
Lettuce and Tomato Salad, Chilled Melon Balls

*Recipe included in this book

Quick and Easy Carrot Cake

Who says carrot cake has to be covered with cream cheese frosting to make it tasty? Try this light and easy alternative.

1/4 cup margarine, softened
1/2 cup sugar
1 egg
1/4 cup low-fat milk
1/2 tsp. vanilla extract
3/4 cup shredded carrots (about 2)
1 cup flour
1 tsp. baking powder
1/4 tsp. cinnamon
1/4 tsp. nutmeg
1 tbsp. confectioners sugar, optional
Vegetable oil cooking spray

Preheat oven to 350°. Cream margarine and sugar until blended. Add egg, milk, vanilla, and carrots. In small bowl, combine flour, baking powder, cinnamon, and nutmeg. Add to carrot mixture. Blend well.

Spray 8" x 8" pan with vegetable oil cooking spray. Pour batter into pan. Bake for approximately 25 minutes until center of cake springs back easily when touched.

Cool. Sprinkle with confectioners sugar, if desired.

Servings: 16
89 calories per serving; 1 gm. protein; 13 gm. carbohydrates;
3 gm. fat; 13 mg. cholesterol; 1 gm. fiber; 0 iron;
11 mg. calcium; 47 mg. sodium

Exchanges:
1/2 bread, 1/2 fruit

*To balance your meal add: *Beef and Broccoli Stir-Fry,
Steamed Rice*

Chewy Chocolate Brownies

You can't get much easier and tastier than these.

Vegetable oil cooking spray
1 cup sugar
1/3 cup margarine, softened
1 tsp. vanilla extract
1 egg
3/4 cup flour
1/4 cup cocoa
1/2 tsp. baking powder

*Recipe included in this book

Glaze (optional):

1/2 cup powdered sugar
1/4 tsp. vanilla extract
1 Tbsp. water

Preheat oven to 350°. Spray 8" x 8" baking pan with vegetable cooking oil spray.

Cream together sugar and margarine. Add vanilla and egg. Add flour, cocoa, and baking powder. Bake 20 minutes or until center springs back easily when touched. Cool.

Drizzle glaze over, if desired.

Servings: 25 brownies
72 calories per brownie, (80 with glaze); 1 gm. (1 gm.) protein;
11 gm. (13 gm.) carbohydrates; 3 gm. (3 gm.) fat;
8 mg. (8 mg.) cholesterol; 0 fiber; 0 iron;
4 mg. (4 mg.) calcium; 31 mg. (31 mg.) sodium

Exchanges:
1/2 fruit

*To balance your meal add: *South of the Border Hash*

Recipe included in this book

Peanut Butter Oatmeal Cookies

1 cup margarine
3/4 cup sugar
3/4 cup brown sugar
1 tsp. vanilla extract
1 cup creamy peanut butter
2 eggs, beaten
1 1/2 cups flour
1 cup bran
3/4 cup rolled oats
2 tsp. baking soda

Preheat oven to 350°. Melt margarine. Combine margarine with sugars, vanilla, peanut butter, and eggs. Beat until smooth. Add flour, bran, oats, and baking soda. Blend until smooth. Drop batter by teaspoons onto ungreased cookie sheet. Bake approximately 15 minutes until golden brown.

Servings: 7 dozen cookies
65 calories per cookie; 1 gm. protein; 7 gm. carbohydrates;
4 gm. fat; 5 mg. cholesterol; 1 gm. fiber; 0 iron;
5 mg. calcium; 62 mg. sodium

Exchanges:
1/2 bread, 1/2 fruit, 1/2 fat (for 2 cookies)

*To balance your meal add: *Quick Sloppy Joes,
Chilled Fruit Cocktail*

Recipe included in this book

Chocolate Oatmeal Cookies

1 cup margarine, softened
3/4 cup firmly packed brown sugar
3/4 cup sugar
1 egg
1 tsp. vanilla extract
1 1/2 cups flour
1 tsp. baking soda
1/2 tsp. salt
1/2 tsp. nutmeg
1 tsp. cinnamon
2 cups uncooked oats
1 cup chocolate chips

Preheat oven to 375°. Cream margarine and sugars. Add egg, vanilla, flour, baking soda, salt, nutmeg, and cinnamon. Blend well. Stir in oats and chocolate chips. Drop batter by teaspoonfuls onto ungreased cookie sheet. Bake 8 minutes. Cool.

Servings: 6 dozen cookies
67 calories per cookie; 1 gm. protein; 9 gm. carbohydrates;
3 gm. fat; 3 mg. cholesterol; 0 fiber; 0 iron;
5 mg. calcium; 58 mg. sodium

Exchanges:
1/2 fruit

To balance your meal add: *Chili and Corn, Low-fat Milk

*Recipe included in this book

Easy Apple Cake

Involve kids—they'll enjoy eating it even more!

3 apples, peeled and chopped
1 tsp. cinnamon
1 1/2 cups flour
1 cup sugar
1 1/2 tsp. baking powder
1/2 cup vegetable oil
2 eggs
2 tbsp. orange juice
1 1/2 tsp. vanilla extract
Vegetable oil cooking spray

Preheat oven to 350°. Sprinkle chopped apples with cinnamon. Set aside. Combine flour, sugar, and baking powder in large bowl. Mix in oil, eggs, orange juice, and vanilla. Add apples. Pour into 8" x 8" pan sprayed with vegetable oil cooking spray. Bake 35-40 minutes or until lightly browned.

Servings: 16 pieces
177 calories per serving; 2 gm. protein; 25 gm. carbohydrates;
8 gm. fat; 26 mg. cholesterol; 1 gm. fiber; 1 mg. iron;
8 mg. calcium; 8 mg. sodium

Exchanges:
1/2 bread, 1 fruit, 1 1/2 fat

*To balance your meal add: *Hamburger Pie*

Apple Pudding

*A dessert that's wholesome, nutritious, and sure to please,
especially on a cool night.*

1 cup flour
3/4 cup sugar
1 tsp. baking soda
1 tsp. cinnamon
1/2 tsp. cloves
3 tbsp. margarine, melted
1 egg, beaten
3 large apples, peeled and chopped
Vegetable oil cooking spray

Preheat oven to 350°. Combine flour, sugar, soda, cinnamon, and cloves. Stir in melted margarine and egg. Add chopped apples. Pour batter into 9" x 9" pan sprayed with vegetable oil cooking spray. Bake 45 minutes. Serve warm.

Servings: 9
183 calories per serving; 2 gm. protein; 34 gm. carbohydrates;
5 gm. fat; 24 mg. cholesterol; 1 gm. fiber; 1 mg. iron;
12 mg. calcium; 144 mg. sodium

Exchanges:
1 bread, 1 1/2 fruit

*To balance your meal add: *Garlic Chicken Stir-Fry, Rice Pilaf*

*Recipe included in this book

Homemade Chocolate Pudding
(Microwave)

Pudding doesn't have to be instant out of a box.
Try making your own.

3 tbsp. sugar
2 tbsp. cocoa
1 tbsp. cornstarch
1 cup low-fat milk
1/4 tsp. vanilla extract

Combine sugar, cocoa, and cornstarch in glass bowl. Add milk, stirring to mix thoroughly.

Microwave mixture on medium-high for 3 minutes, stopping to stir halfway through. Mixture should thicken as it cooks.

Stir vanilla into mixture. Pour into pudding cups. Refrigerate about 10 minutes until chilled.

Servings: 2 (1/2 cup each)
162 calories per serving; 5 gm. protein; 31 gm. carbohydrates;
3 gm. fat; 9 mg. cholesterol; 2 gm. fiber; 1 mg. iron;
155 mg. calcium; 62 mg. sodium

Exchanges:
1/2 bread, 1 fruit, 1/2 milk, 1/2 fat

To balance your meal add: *Easy Mexican Potato,
Steamed Broccoli

*Recipe included in this book

No-Cook Applesauce

*Enjoy autumn by taking your family apple picking
and making homemade applesauce.*

4 apples, peeled and chopped
1/4 cup lemon juice
1 tbsp. plus 1 tsp. sugar
1/2 tsp. cinnamon
1/2 tsp. nutmeg

Combine apples and lemon juice in food processor. Blend until smooth. If necessary, add several drops of water to help blend. Stir in the sugar and spices.

Servings: 4 (3/4 cup)
95 calories per serving; 0 protein; 24 gm. carbohydrates;
0 fat; 0 cholesterol; 3 gm. fiber; 0 iron;
11 mg. calcium; 3 mg. sodium

Exchanges:
1 1/2 fruit

*To balance your meal add: *Chick 'n Pepper Stir-Fry,
Steamed Couscous*

*Recipe included in this book

Bird's Nest Cookies

Children love to make their own nests and choose the color of jelly beans to use for eggs. This is definitely a recipe for "hands-on" involvement of children, even pre-school age.

6-oz. package butterscotch or peanut butter morsels
2 tbsp. peanut butter
3-oz. package chow mein noodles
8-oz. package jelly beans

Melt morsels and peanut butter in saucepan over low heat. Stir in noodles. Mix until well coated. Place a tablespoon of noodles on waxed paper. Shape into a nest with a large spoon. Add jelly beans for eggs.

Servings: 12 (2 small cookies)
98 calories per serving; 1 gm. protein; 16 gm. carbohydrates;
4 gm. fat; 0 cholesterol; 0 fiber; 0 iron;
4 mg. calcium; 31 mg. sodium

Exchanges:
1 fruit, 1/2 fat

*To balance your meal add: *Ratatouille Potato*

*Recipe included in this book

Danish Apple Pie
(Microwave)

Need dessert in a hurry? Here's the answer.

7 cooking apples, peeled, cored, and sliced
3/4 cup sugar
2 tbsp. flour
1/8 tsp. salt
1 tsp. cinnamon
1 baked 9-inch pie shell
2 tbsp. margarine
1/4 cup flour
1/4 cup brown sugar

Place apples in large mixing bowl. Combine sugar, flour, salt, and cinnamon. Add to apples and toss to coat. Pour apples into pie shell, placed in microwave-safe pie dish.

In small bowl, cut margarine into flour and brown sugar. Sprinkle over apples. Cook on high for 12-14 minutes, until apples are tender when poked with a fork. Cool before serving.

*Recipe included in this book

Servings: 8 (3/4 cup)

321 calories per serving; 2 gm. protein; 57 gm. carbohydrates;
10 gm. fat; 0 cholesterol; 3 gm. fiber; 1 mg. iron;
31 mg. calcium; 226 mg. sodium

Exchanges:
1 bread, 3 fruit, 2 fat

*To balance your meal add: *Homemade Chicken Nuggets,
Steamed String Beans, Low-fat Milk*

Gingersnaps

1 cup sugar, divided
2 1/4 cups flour
2/3 cup oil
1/4 cup molasses
1/4 cup maple syrup
2 tsp. baking soda
1 tsp. ginger
1/2 tsp. cinnamon
1/2 tsp. nutmeg
1/4 tsp. salt
1 egg

Preheat oven to 325°. In large bowl, combine 1/2 cup sugar and remaining ingredients. Blend well. Take 1 tablespoon of batter at a time and roll it into a ball. Roll in remaining 1/2 cup sugar. Place cookies on ungreased cookie sheet. Flatten balls slightly with the backside of a fork. Bake 8 minutes.

Servings: 3 1/2 dozen cookies
85 calories per cookie; 1 gm. protein; 13 gm. carbohydrates;
4 gm. fat; 5 mg. cholesterol; 0 fiber; 0 iron;
7 mg. calcium; 54 mg. sodium

Exchanges:
1/2 bread, 1/2 fruit, 1/2 fat

*To balance your meal add: *Ground Beef Fajitas,*
Fresh Tomato Slices
Recipe included in this book

Peanut Butter Pudding

This pudding will surely please your little ones.

1/3 cup sugar

2 tbsp. cornstarch

2 cups low-fat milk

1/4 cup creamy peanut butter

1 tsp. vanilla extract

2 egg whites

1/4 tsp. salt

2 tbsp. sugar

Chopped peanuts, nondairy whipped topping, optional

In medium saucepan, combine 1/3 cup sugar with cornstarch. Slowly add milk. Bring to boil. Cook for 1 minute, stirring constantly, until mixture thickens. Remove from heat. Add peanut butter and vanilla.

Beat egg whites and salt until frothy. Gradually add 2 tbsp. sugar, beating until stiff, but not dry.

Fold egg whites into peanut butter mixture. Pour into serving dishes. Cover and chill. Garnish with chopped peanuts and whipped topping, if desired.

Servings: 6 (1/2 cup each)
180 calories per serving; 6 gm. protein; 24 gm. carbohydrates;
7 gm. fat; 6 mg. cholesterol; 1 gm. fiber; 0 iron;
103 mg. calcium; 198 mg. sodium

Exchanges:
1/2 meat, 1 fruit, 1/2 milk, 1 fat

*To balance your meal add: *Barbecue Chicken and Rice*

Strawberry Sorbet

*Dress up your dinner with this elegant but easy sorbet. You'll need
a little time to allow for freezing, but it's worth the wait.*

1/2 cup sugar
2/3 cup water
2 1/2 pints (5 cups) fresh strawberries
2 tbsp. lemon juice
Fresh strawberry halves

In medium saucepan, combine sugar and water. Bring to boil. Boil
until sugar dissolves, stirring constantly. Remove from heat. Cool.

Recipe included in this book

Puree strawberries in food processor or blender. Press strawberry puree through sieve or several layers of cheesecloth to extract juice. Discard pulp.

Combine sugar, water, strawberry juice, and lemon juice. Pour mixture into freezer tray or 8-inch square pan and freeze until almost firm.

Break mixture into food processor bowl. Process several seconds until fluffy, but not thawed. Return to freezer. Freeze until firm.

Use ice cream scoop to serve. Garnish with fresh strawberry halves.

Servings: 6 (1/2 cup each)
102 calories per serving; 1 gm. protein; 25 gm. carbohydrates;
0 fat; 0 cholesterol; 3 gm. fiber; 0 iron;
18 mg. calcium; 2 mg. sodium

Exchanges:
1 1/2 fruit

*To balance your meal add: *Golden Baked Fish Fillet,
Oven Fried Potato Duet, Low-fat Milk

Recipe included in this book

213

Rainbow Fruit Sticks

Try any type of fruit with this recipe. Use your imagination.
Children can make their own rainbow with fruits,
and even vegetables, of their choice.

1/2 cup strawberries
1/2 cup blueberries
1/2 cup red seedless grapes
1/2 cup green seedless grapes
1/2 cup mandarin orange slices
6 long toothpicks

Place fruit on toothpicks to look like a rainbow. Continue
doing so until you use up all the fruit.

Servings: 6 (1 stick)
32 calories per serving; 0 protein; 8 gm. carbohydrates;
0 fat; 0 cholesterol; 1 gm. fiber; 0 iron;
7 mg. calcium; 2 mg. sodium

Exchanges:
1/2 fruit

To balance your meal add: *Western Beef Casserole

*Recipe included in this book

Kid-
Approved
Snacks
and
Lunch
Treats

Kid Snacks

nacks are an important part of a diet and should be planned as such. They should be designed to complement other choices made throughout the day.

Small children require snacks as part of their daily intake because their small tummies just can't take in enough food in 3 meals. Snacks for these children should almost be considered as "mini meals." Older children who learn to enjoy healthy snacks right from the start will favor healthier choices once they make their own choices at school and at play. And, of course, parents should set a good example for their families by selecting healthful snacks for themselves and when purchasing foods to bring into the home.

Try these quick snack foods to satisfy your in-between meal hunger:

air popped popcorn with Parmesan cheese

pretzels, hard or soft

breadsticks

mini bagels

rice cakes

raisin bread

low-fat tortilla chips with salsa

dry low-sugar cereal

graham crackers

apple slices

dried fruit
cucumber slices
fresh red, green or yellow pepper slices
baby carrots
cherry tomatoes
yogurt raisins
fig bars
gingersnaps
oatmeal cookies
animal crackers
vanilla wafers
yogurt
low-fat pudding
frozen yogurt

or, if you are feeling creative, have some fun with your kids and make your own snacks.

Your Own Chips

Most everyone loves chips. Have fun and make your own. You can even put together a combination of chips for your next party or family gathering.

Pita Chips

Split large pita bread into 2 circles. Cut each circle into 8 wedges. Toast wedges on a cookie sheet at 325° for 8 minutes or until crisp.

Servings: 2 (8 chips)
82 calories per serving; 3 gm. protein; 17 gm. carbohydrates;
0 fat; 0 cholesterol; 0 fiber; 1 mg. iron;
26 mg. calcium; 161 mg. sodium

Exchanges:
1 bread

Tortilla Chips

Cut tortilla into 6 wedges. Toast on cookie sheet at 400° for 10-12 minutes or until crisp.

Servings: 1 (6 chips)
115 calories per serving; 3 gm. protein; 20 gm. carbohydrates;
2 gm. fat; 0 cholesterol; 1 gm. fiber; 1 mg. iron;
44 mg. calcium; 169 mg. sodium

Exchanges:
1 bread

Bagel Chips

Slice one or two day-old bagels into slices 1/4" thick. Toast on cookie sheet at 350° for 10-12 minutes until crisp.

Servings: 2 (3 chips)
93 calories per serving; 3 gm. protein; 18 gm. carbohydrates;
0 fat; 0 cholesterol; 1 gm. fiber; 1 mg. iron;
25 mg. calcium; 182 mg. sodium

Exchanges:
1 bread

Easy Vegetable Dip

This dip will definitely help you get your children to eat their veggies. You'll like it too.

1 cup low-fat cottage cheese
1/2 of 8-oz. container soft-style cream cheese
   with onion and chives
1 tsp. dried dillweed

Blend cottage cheese in blender until smooth. Add cream cheese and dillweed. Blend. Pour into serving dish. Place in refrigerator until ready to serve. Serve with fresh raw vegetables.

Servings: 8 (3 tablespoons each)
76 calories per serving; 4 gm. protein; 2 gm. carbohydrates;
6 gm. fat; 17 mg. cholesterol; 0 fiber; 0 iron;
38 mg. calcium; 166 mg. sodium

Exchanges:
1/2 meat, 1 fat

Pretzel Dip

This is also a great dip for fresh, raw vegetable and fruit slices, too.

2 tbsp. peanut butter
3 tbsp. carrot, finely grated
3 tbsp. applesauce
2-oz. pretzel sticks

Mix together the peanut butter, carrots, and applesauce. Let children scoop the dip onto the pretzel sticks.

Servings: 4 (2 tablespoons each)
108 calories per serving; 3 gm. protein; 15 gm. carbohydrates;
4 gm. fat; 0 cholesterol; 1 gm. fiber; 1 mg. iron;
9 mg. calcium; 283 mg. sodium

Exchanges:
1/2 bread, 1/2 fat

Frozen Yogurt Sandwiches

Make a batch of these to wrap and freeze.
They'll be ready when you are.

2 graham cracker squares
2 tbsp. frozen yogurt, any flavor

Spread softened frozen yogurt between 2 graham cracker squares. Squeeze together to make sandwich. Eat immediately or put in freezer for later.

Servings: 1 sandwich
58 calories per serving; 1 gm. protein; 10 gm. carbohydrates;
2 gm. fat; 0 cholesterol; 0 fiber; 0 iron;
27 mg. calcium; 58 mg. sodium

Exchanges:
1/2 bread

Soft Pretzels

A fun snack to make and to eat. Try different shapes, letters, or knots for variety.

1 (1/4-oz.) package dry yeast
1 1/2 cups warm water
1 tsp. salt
1 tbsp. sugar
4 cups flour
1 egg, beaten
Coarse salt

Preheat oven to 425°. In large metal bowl, dissolve yeast in warm water. Add salt, sugar, and flour. Knead until smooth.

Cut dough into small pieces, about 1" in diameter. Roll into long skinny strips. Twist into pretzel shapes. Place pretzels onto greased cookie sheet. Brush with egg and sprinkle with coarse salt.

Bake for 15 minutes until golden brown.

Servings: 24 pretzels
82 calories per pretzel; 2 gm. protein; 17 gm. carbohydrates;
0 fat; 9 mg. cholesterol; 1 gm. fiber; 1 mg. iron;
4 mg. calcium; 92 mg. sodium

Exchanges:
1 bread

Applesauce Cake Cones

Let your children help fill the cones.

1/4 cup vegetable oil
3/4 cup firmly packed brown sugar
1 cup applesauce
1 tsp. baking soda
1 1/2 cups unsifted whole wheat flour
1 tsp. cinnamon
10 flat-bottomed ice cream cones
Peanut butter, cream cheese, nuts, raisins, optional

Preheat oven to 375°. Mix oil and sugar together. Add applesauce, baking soda, flour, and cinnamon. Stir well. Fill cones 1/2-3/4 full with batter. Bake on cookie sheet for about 20 minutes. Top with peanut butter, low-fat cream cheese, nuts, or raisins. Or eat without a topping at all!

Servings: 10
197 calories per cone; 3 gm. protein; 33 gm. carbohydrates;
6 gm. fat; 0 cholesterol; 3 gm. fiber; 1 mg. iron;
21 mg. calcium; 18 mg. sodium

Exchanges:
1 bread, 1 fruit, 1 fat

Peanut Butter Play Dough

This recipe is especially good for kids who like to play with their food. Best of all, when they're done playing, they can eat it.

1/2 cup peanut butter
1 tsp. honey
1/4 cup dry milk powder

Combine all ingredients in small bowl. Mix thoroughly. If batter is too sticky, add more milk powder. If it is too dry, add more honey. Play and eat.

Servings: enough for 2 children to play
104 calories per tablespoon; 5 gm. protein; 5 gm. carbohydrates;
8 gm. fat; 0 cholesterol; 1 gm. fiber; 0 iron;
32 mg. calcium; 88 mg. sodium

Exchanges:
1/2 meat, 1/2 fruit, 1 fat

Homemade Granola

There are many variations to this recipes.
It's delicious, nutritious, and easy to pack and take anywhere.

2 cups dry quick cooking oats
1/4 tsp. salt
1/4 cup honey
1/2 cup wheat germ
2 tbsp. vegetable oil
1/4 cup raisins
1/4 cup dates
1/4 cup peanuts
1/4 cup sunflower seeds
(Try adding dried apricots, peaches, apples, banana
     chips, grated coconuts, and other nuts for variety.)

Preheat oven to 250°. Combine oats, salt, honey, wheat germ, and oil. Spread mixture onto an ungreased cookie sheet. Bake 30 minutes, stirring once. Remove from oven. Stir in remaining ingredients. Bake additional 15 minutes. Remove from oven. Let cool. Store in glass jar with a tight lid. Refrigerate until ready to eat.

Servings: 10 (1/2 cup each)
191 calories per serving; 5 gm. protein; 27 gm. carbohydrates;
8 gm. fat; 0 cholesterol; 3 gm. fiber; 1 mg. iron;
22 mg. calcium; 56 mg. sodium

Exchanges:
1/2 bread, 1 fruit, 1 fat

Dog Bones (for kids)

This is a great after school activity because children of all ages can participate and create their own shapes and sizes.

1/2 cup smooth peanut butter
1/2 cup dry milk powder
1 tbsp. honey
2 large graham crackers, crushed

In small bowl, combine peanut butter and dry milk. Add honey and mix well. (It will be stiff.) Divide into 6 balls. Mold each piece into the shape of a dog bone (or any creative shape you choose.)

Crush graham crackers in a resealable bag using a rolling pin. Sprinkle graham cracker crumbs on both sides of the dog bones. Enjoy.

Servings: 6
182 calories per bone; 9 gm. protein; 14 gm. carbohydrates;
11 gm. fat; 2 mg. cholesterol; 1 gm. fiber; 0 iron;
134 mg. calcium; 169 mg. sodium

Exchanges:
1/2 meat, 1/2 fruit, 1 1/2 fat

Wheat Germ Peanut Butter Balls

This is a great recipe for a group of children. Allow them to select and measure ingredients and help with mixing.

1 cup peanut butter, smooth or chunky
1/2 cup sesame seeds
1/2 cup dry oats
1/2 cup honey
1/2 cup sunflower seeds
1/2 cup dry milk powder
1/2 cup raisins
1/2 cup water (use only enough to hold together)
1/2 cup wheat germ

Combine all ingredients, except wheat germ, in large bowl. Form into balls. Roll each ball in wheat germ. Refrigerate until ready to eat.

Servings: 36 balls
100 calories per ball; 4 gm. protein; 10 gm. carbohydrates;
6 gm. fat; 0 cholesterol; 1 gm. fiber; 1 mg. iron;
30 mg. calcium; 44 mg. sodium

Exchanges:
1/2 fruit, 1 fat

Thirst

Quenchers

Spiced Tea

Put the kids to bed and relax with a cup of hot spiced tea.
There's nothing better at the end of a long day.

6 cups water
1 tsp. cloves
1 cinnamon stick
3 tea bags
1/2 cup sugar
3/4 cup orange juice
1 tbsp. lemon juice

Combine water, cloves, and cinnamon in medium saucepan or tea pot. Bring to boil. Remove from heat. Add tea bags to water and steep for 10 minutes. Remove cloves, cinnamon, and tea bags.

In small saucepan combine sugar and orange and lemon juice. Bring to boil. Combine juice mixture and tea in pitcher. Serve hot or over ice. Refrigerate remainder.

Servings: 6 (1 cup)
81 calories per serving; 0 protein; 20 gm. carbohydrates;
0 fat; 0 cholesterol; 0 fiber; 0 iron;
6 mg. calcium; 5 mg. sodium

Exchanges:
1 1/2 fruit

Banana Berry Smoothie Oozie

Great as a breakfast drink or snack.

2 bananas
2 cups strawberries
1 cup low-fat milk
1 cup low-fat plain yogurt

Peel and slice bananas. Wash and cut off tops of strawberries. Combine bananas, strawberries, milk, and yogurt into blender and blend until smooth. Do not overblend and the mixture will stay thick.

Servings: 4 (1 cup each)
142 calories per serving; 6 gm. protein; 26 gm. carbohydrates;
3 gm. fat; 8 mg. cholesterol; 3 gm. fiber; 1 mg. iron;
199 mg. calcium; 74 mg. sodium

Exchanges:
1 fruit, 1/2 milk, 1/2 fat

Fruity Slurpie

*Here's a thirst-quenching treat for a warm day.
It's fun to make and fun to eat.*

3 oranges
3 lemons
3 bananas
3 cups water
1 cup sugar

Squeeze juice from oranges and lemons. Peel and mash bananas.
Combine juices with bananas in mixing bowl. Add water and
sugar. Mix well. Put bowl in freezer. Stir well twice during a one-
hour period. Return to freezer after stirring. Serve when icy but
not frozen solid.

Servings: 6 (1 cup)
195 calories per serving; 1 gm. protein; 50 gm. carbohydrates;
0 fat; 0 cholesterol; 1 gm. fiber; 0 iron;
7 mg. calcium; 1 mg. sodium

Exchanges:
3 fruit

Dreamsicle Milkshake

Vanilla and orange make a delicious combination.
Here's a frozen treat that's refreshing and nourishing.

3 cups low-fat milk
3/4 cup vanilla frozen yogurt
6-oz. can frozen orange juice concentrate

Combine all ingredients in blender. Blend until smooth. Serve.

Servings: 4 (1 cup each)
198 calories per serving; 9 gm. protein; 32 gm. carbohydrates;
4 gm. fat; 17 mg. cholesterol; 0 fiber; 0 iron;
283 mg. calcium; 111 mg. sodium

Exchanges:
1 1/2 fruit, 1 milk, 1 fat

Frozen Strawberry Treat

*Absolutely delicious. Easy to make and what a treat!
It's so thick you can eat it with a spoon.*

1 cup frozen unsweetened strawberries
1 cup low-fat plain yogurt or buttermilk

Combine ingredients in blender and blend until smooth. (If using buttermilk, you may want to add 2 tsp. sugar to mixture.)

Servings: 2 (1 cup each)
103 calories per serving; 7 gm. protein; 15 gm. carbohydrates;
2 gm. fat; 7 mg. cholesterol; 2 gm. fiber; 1 mg. iron;
235 mg. calcium; 87 mg. sodium

Exchanges:
1/2 fruit, 1/2 milk

Index

G

N

O

P